UNASHAMEDLY
SUPERHUMAN

UNASHAMEDLY SUPERHUMAN

HARNESS YOUR INNER POWER AND ACHIEVE YOUR GREATEST PROFESSIONAL AND PERSONAL GOALS

JIM STEELE

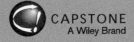

CAPSTONE
A Wiley Brand

Registered office
John Wiley & Sons Ltd, The Atrium, Southern Gate, Chichester, West Sussex, PO19 8SQ, United Kingdom

John Wiley & Sons, Inc., 111 River Street, Hoboken, NJ 07030, USA

Wiley-VCH GmbH, Boschstr. 12, 69469 Weinheim, Germany

John Wiley & Sons Singapore Pte. Ltd, 1 Fusionopolis Walk, #06-01 Solaris South Tower, Singapore 138628

Editorial Office
John Wiley & Sons Ltd, The Atrium, Southern Gate, Chichester, West Sussex, PO19 8SQ, United Kingdom

For details of our global editorial offices, customer services, and more information about Wiley products visit us at www.wiley.com.

Wiley also publishes its books in a variety of electronic formats and by print-on-demand. Some content that appears in standard print versions of this book may not be available in other formats.

Library of Congress Cataloging-in-Publication Data

Names: Steele, Jim, author.
Title: Unashamedly superhuman : harness your inner power and achieve your
    greatest professional and personal goals / Jim Steele.
Description: Hoboken, NJ : Wiley-Capstone, 2023. | Includes index.
Identifiers: LCCN 2022025464 (print) | LCCN 2022025465 (ebook) | ISBN
    9781119828518 (paperback) | ISBN 9781119828532 (adobe pdf) | ISBN
    9781119828525 (epub)
Subjects: LCSH: Success in business. | Well-being. | Work-life balance.
Classification: LCC HF5386 .S8246 2023 (print) | LCC HF5386 (ebook) | DDC
    650.1—dc23/eng/20220728
LC record available at https://lccn.loc.gov/2022025464
LC ebook record available at https://lccn.loc.gov/2022025465

Cover Design and Image: Wiley

Set in 10/13 pt ITC NewBaskervilleStd-Roman by Straive, Chennai, India
Printed and bound by CPI Group (UK) Ltd, Croydon, CR0 4YY

C9781119828518_180822

Contents

Foreword

My name is Oliver Medill. Like the author, I am a speaker, a business coach, and an author. I worked with Jim at Speakers International, latterly RogenSi, for several years. Like Jim, I too moved on to set up my own consultancy and have been lucky enough to work with him on many occasions in the years since our early adventures at "Speakers."

Our friendship started with a shared passion for human development, and we have spent many transatlantic flights discussing various strategies whilst our fellow passengers snored around us. It has been enhanced in later years by a shared fondness for aspiring golf and pinot noir!

My first impression of Jim – an enigma; a mysterious blend of laid-back and acutely perceptive at the same time. A little detached from the everyday hurly-burly of a busy agency, he would observe his co-workers through a filter of curiosity and a sense of the ridiculous – sometimes surprised by something new, sometimes convinced of an earlier theory, but always entertained by what he saw.

I realised gradually that Jim was, rightly, revered as a speaker because of this quirky view on life and human behaviour. Not automatically convinced by commonly held dogma, he would always filter both well-known practical advice and thorough research through his amused, questing view of the world. The resulting conclusions, rigorously saved for his talks and articles, never for mundane day-to-day conversation, appeared like freshly-minted coins – bright, new, inviting closer inspection, and above all, profoundly useful.

Always energetic, always amusing, it might be easy to think of Jim as just a performer, an entertainer. But this would be doing him a disservice.

The beguiling, laid-back facade hid a raging and perpetual hunger for new insights and a burning desire to turn these insights into easy-to-use strategies. The man believes in and cares deeply about his work and about the audiences he speaks to, whether in person or now, in his first book.

The result? Dynamite.

I feel both flattered and proud to have been asked to write these few words about *Unashamedly Superhuman*. I gobbled it up. You will find it, in turns, a fascinating and entertaining read. Chatty and conversational, *Unashamedly Superhuman* is a heady cocktail of personal experiences, ground-breaking research, and personally experienced advice. A study of *human* development, *Unashamedly Superhuman* transcends the line effortlessly between the personal and the professional; a win-win.

The book is a journey in two senses. First, Jim's journey of discovery – an experiential adventure of pushing himself beyond the limits of what one would normally expect people to endure. Second, the journey of discovery that Jim invites the reader to travel with him. The first journey is a highly entertaining blend of self-deprecation, surprise, and astonishment of what he has been able to achieve; the second is a masterful distillation of cutting-edge "how tos," or "hacks," explained with clarity and reinforced with hard data.

After the scene-setting opening section, there are three areas of focus:

> **BETTER**, which taps into expanding our potential; watch out for the story Jim tells about his experience in Hong Kong, where common sense and the power of re-framing triumphs over common practice.
>
> **SMARTER**, which explores the power of mindset. The line "Strategies, not straplines" sticks in the mind. Look out for the "business card" exercise around purpose too—a game-changer.

STRONGER, which offers fascinating tips for using the untapped power of the body to maximise its power and, fascinatingly, for recharging—or recovery. I was particularly drawn to the point that different parts of the day are better for different activities to recharge the body (look out for *active* recovery and *micro*-recovery).

There are different reasons why *Unashamedly Superhuman* is a must-read. To begin with, unlike so many books in this field, the many "hacks" for attaining the eponymous superhuman qualities have been hard-earned by the author himself. This isn't just theory or research.

Next, in my 20 years of knowing and working with Jim, he has, without exception, proved his mantra that every project he works on is the most important thing in his existence, whether it is delivering a speech, hosting a conference, completing an IRONMAN® triathlon, or writing a book. I know how important this value is to him from personal experience and *Unashamedly Superhuman* is no exception.

And last, I want to coin one of Jim's favourite phrases: "This only works." Again, from personal experience I know that every word in his book is about strategies that *work*. There is no fluff or filler. It only works.

Whatever your BHAG (Big Hairy Audacious Goal – mentioned throughout), *Unashamedly Superhuman* is your key to reaching it, using your newly accessed potential, your re-wired mindset, and finally, by following the many "hacks" for empowered physiology and for recovery.

If you apply the learning, this book will change your life.

Oliver Medill
Founder and Managing Director of All
About Impact and Author of *The Impact Formula*

Acknowledgments

I'll start at the beginning. The wheels started turning when Stacey Winters floated the idea that high performance and well-being could be interlinked. To my many clients and collaborators for the opportunities to test the content in the real world: Natural Direction, Open Water, Axis, and the team at the London Speaker Bureau to name a few. Special thanks to James Poole at the Gordon Poole Agency for posing the all-important question, "Have you thought about writing a book?" Bonus points for then introducing me to Annie Knight and the team at Wiley.

Hey, Oliver. Thank you. Yes, for your most generous Foreword, but more for the quarterly rounds of golf that always provoke quality conversation and, in spite of my scorecard, never fail to lift my spirits.

A heartfelt thanks for the opportunity to be a part of the Three Amigos and the Four Musketeers. You have held a high bar for more than two decades. The challenge has always been appreciated.

To my family, past and present. The ups and downs, ins and outs, back and forths have been the best of all testing grounds for the content herein. It's been an adventure. You provide a safety net that has enabled me to wander off into the unknown. Let's just say WALES! WALES! WALES!

One thing that connects training for an endurance event and writing a book is the selfish nature of these pursuits. A great misconception is that these solo journeys require our sacrifice alone. Of course, that couldn't be further from the truth. Those nearest to us often put their goals on hold in order to facilitate ours. My partner in crime, Julia, most certainly did. For two years I pretty much disappeared. Whether into a seven-day-a-week training schedule or down one of many rabbit holes, while in the struggle phase of writing, the support I received was unconditional throughout.

If I listed out the many ways in which you contributed, we'd be deep into another chapter. Suffice it to say, I couldn't have completed and finished either of these BHAGs without you.

And finally to my girls, Tirian and Manon. I may have started typing *Unashamedly Superhuman* a year ago, but it really started in 1992. Becoming a father inspired the need in me to try to work this shit out. If it makes sense, pass it on.

It's my adventurers guide for Sebi, et al.♥

Introduction

Full disclosure: I am not (and have never been) a superhero. I am, however, proud to call myself *Unashamedly Superhuman*. More about what that term really means in Chapter 1, but for now, it's enough to know that you too can become *Unashamedly Superhuman*. You have the potential to be and do more. This book, more than anything, is about tapping into your potential and performing at your highest level.

Over the course of the following chapters, I want to introduce you to parts of yourself you didn't even know existed. I'm talking about your inner resources that you've always had but maybe not always accessed. Some of you might have used them in the past, but often when we tap into our superhuman side it's not by design but by necessity. What I've learned is that you do have a sense of control over when and how you access your superhuman abilities, and I'll share how as we move through this book.

These are not haphazard, chance abilities. These are abilities you can predict, determine, and turn towards any area of your life that will benefit from you being *Unashamedly Superhuman*. You can use your inner powers to help you achieve your greatest personal and professional goals. Sound too good to be true?

I know, I was cynical at first as well. I had always believed that I had to sacrifice my well-being for performance. It was a simple trade-off in my mind, as I imagine it is in yours. But then I was set a challenge to combine the two, which threw me into uncharted territory. Sink or swim. Ultimately, this resulted in me becoming better, smarter, and stronger than I ever had been before.

It turns out well-being is a key enabler for performance and one of the keys to tapping into your superhuman abilities is to treat recovery as a performance strategy. As someone who has always been excited by performance, this lit a spark.

No magic required . . .

I'm in New York City. It's 9 a.m. and the first speaker is about to open the conference. I'm booked to close the event at 4 p.m. There are 2,000 delegates waiting with anticipation. The theme of the event is, "Creating Magical Results." Fittingly, the opening speaker was a world-famous magician. It would add a bit of spice to tell you who, but it would actually detract from the point. You'll see why shortly.

His mind-boggling routine of misdirection and sleight of hand will set the scene for the day. How to create magical results as sales professionals. Nice analogy. Cheesy, but nice.

It was December 1998. My first ever professional engagement in the United States. Here I was watching from the side-lines, transfixed as the master thrilled his audience with smoke and mirrors. It struck me that as I was standing behind him, at the side of the stage, surely from this advantageous perspective, I'd see something that the audience wouldn't, thus revealing what we all know, deep down, there is no magic . . . just strategy!

I narrowed my eyes and focused on his every move. "For my final illusion," he said, "I will read someone's mind." Body language can reveal a tremendous amount about the thoughts and emotions someone is experiencing, but the ability to actually read another person's thoughts, I don't think so.

So, the volunteer came on stage and we're shown the deck of cards on a huge screen via a live link camera. The volunteer, Sandy, is given the cards. She cuts them, cuts them again, and removes the top card. All the while the magician's back is turned. He couldn't have seen it. I was 10 feet (3 metres) away. Sandy pockets the selected card just to be sure.

The magic man turns around, stands opposite Sandy, and looks deep into her eyes. "Don't speak or try to help me in any way. Just think of the card and picture it in your mind . . . ."

Looking intently at every pore on Sandy's face he states confidently, "It's a black card."

A pause. "It's a spade." Another pause, "I think I've got it," he says. No way, I'm thinking. Not possible. He commits, "Nine of Spades."

Sandy reaches into her pocket and holds up her card for all to see. The nine of spades. The audience erupts into applause. A standing ovation follows as the magic man exits stage right. He sees me looking. He avoids eye contact as he strides past me. "That was amazing," I enthused. No response. Not a nod, not a smile. I figured I had nothing to lose.

"How did you do the last one?" I asked. "Why do you want to know?" he replied. Still no eye contact, "You're not just curious are you?" I thought that was an unusual question, and I replied that I was really, really interested in knowing his secret.

I guess the point behind his question was that there was no point telling me how to do the trick unless I had the ability and the intention of actually doing it. I assured him I would. After some umming and ahhing he did indeed show me and now I'm going to show you. When I do, you'll say it's the best card trick you've ever seen. You'll also know that anyone can do it. No skills required. Finally, you'll know why it works 100 percent of the time.

Scan the QR code and all will be revealed. Note: Only do this if you're sure you'll do the trick to one person within the next month.

So, you now know how to do the "trick." You know that it requires just five minutes' preparation, minimal practice, and the success rate is 100 percent.

Most important of all, you now know for sure that to create magical results you don't need luck or mysterious powers, you just need a damn good, foolproof strategy.

Inspired by the great and the good

One of the most rewarding aspects of my role as a speaker and performance consultant is the opportunity I have to work with and interview a wide range of fascinating people, all with their own take on what it takes to succeed in their given field.

From the business world, Virgin's Richard Branson comes to mind or the UK MD of Brother, Phil Jones. From the world of professional sport, Sir Chris Hoy or Olympic Hockey captain Kate Richardson-Walsh. Ollie Phillips, voted world rugby player of the year went on to become a serial adventurer. He sailed a yacht around the world, cycled across America and got into the Guinness book of world records for hosting the most northerly rugby match. At the North Pole! Talking of adventurers, Sir Ranulph Fiennes and Chris Moon had remarkable stories to tell, as did the astronauts Charlie Duke, Buzz Aldrin, and one of the UK's first female fighter pilots and author of *An Officer Not a Gentleman*, Mandy Hickson. Equally, I've taken inspiration and wisdom from observing managers, leaders, and individual contributors from all walks of life, famous or otherwise.

Finally, in my search for combining high performance and well-being, I've lost count of the numerous 'a-ha' moments that I've had along the way. My mind has been blown on more occasions than I care to remember. I've attended seminars and training programmes, and immersed myself in hundreds and hundreds of hours of provocative, insightful, and inspiring long-form podcasts. I've loved every minute; none more so than the work of Dr Michael Gervais, a published, peer-reviewed author and recognized speaker on optimal human performance, and Steven Kotler, the *New York Times* bestselling author, award-winning journalist, and the founder and executive director of the Flow Research Collective. And then there is Professor Andrew Huberman, the American neuroscientist and tenured professor in the Department of Neurobiology at the Stanford University School of Medicine. If I said he has a brain the size of a planet and knows everything about everything, I might be exaggerating, but only slightly. I'll mention him often within the pages of this book and I'll continue to turn to him as my interest in neuroscience deepens.

Enthusiastic lab rat

The insights gathered from all of the above, influenced me greatly.

All, in their own way adding to the rich melting pot of principles, ideas, and techniques that I was happy to dive into. That said, the process of learning, developing and putting into practice the various tools, tips, tricks and hacks tested me greatly. Tested the limits of my abilities for sure, but also on occasion tested my patience. Nobody said 'Superhuman' was going to be easy. It wasn't. It was however an enlightening journey of discovery.

This book is not just about my journey to become *Unashamedly Superhuman*. I invite you to set out on your own journey to achieve that same goal. Your version of *Unashamedly Superhuman* will undoubtedly look different to mine. At its core, this concept is about feeling strong from the inside out. None of us are perfect, but we are all capable of more than we realise. We all have better, smarter, and stronger parts inside us; all we need to know is how to access them.

Part I sets the scene and shows you just how far I've come on my own journey (as well as explaining exactly why I embarked on this particular path in the first place). If you're wondering what *Unashamedly Superhuman* really means, you'll find out in these first two chapters.

Part II of *Unashamedly Superhuman* is titled "BETTER – Tapping into Potential."

Here, we're going to crack the code for how to gain access to some remarkable resources that will enable us to adapt to our surroundings and respond to challenges and opportunities with agility.

Part III is titled "SMARTER – Tapping into Mindset."

In this part we look into our ability to structure our thinking in order to increase confidence and mental focus. We also focus on how to get into the zone and access that super productive state of mind where we both feel and perform at our best. Flow!

Part IV is titled "STRONGER – Tapping into Physiology."

With the chapters in this part, we get underneath our extraordinary capabilities and discover what it takes to build successful habits that ensure we can push ourselves to the edge of our abilities whilst at the same time recover in a truly world class way.

To sum up, *Unashamedly Superhuman* explores the principles, ideas, and strategies that will enable you to combine two critical areas, high performance and well-being.

Let the games begin!

SETTING THE SCENE

Figure I.1 Introducing the author

The left-hand picture in Figure I.1 was taken on 25 April 2018. That'll be me on the left. Large glass of red, Marlborough light, and what can only be described as man boobs. Moobs!

The picture on the right is a still shot taken from a video of me crossing the finishing line on 2 September 2021. Mileage covered totalled 140.6 (226.3 km): 2.4-mile (3.86 km) swim, 112 miles (180.25 km) on the bike, and then a 26.2-mile (42.2-km) marathon. Time taken: 12 hours, 33 minutes. Aesthetically, the vital statistics, externally at least, didn't change much over the 30 months. Maybe a cup size smaller. Internally, however, it's a different story.

My respiratory and cardiovascular systems stats are a world apart. Biomechanics, joints, knees, and back health? Best they've ever been. How do I know? Well, after 12.5 hours and 140 miles I was barely out of breath and totally pain free. Something was responsible for this internal transformation.

Was it the exercise, the transition to barefoot running, the daily breathwork routine, and cold showers? Maybe. Or the nutritional strategy, ditching the traditional methods of fueling with carbohydrates and replacing it with fat, or the personalised approach to hydration? Possibly. Dispatching cigarettes and alcohol for a couple of years probably helped. Or was it the mental rehearsal or the positive self-talk or maybe the rapid de-stress techniques that I picked up from a prof at Stamford that kept me moving forward through the toughest moments? Likely to have helped. Or perhaps the techniques I picked up from the Flow Research Collective for how to drop into the Zone, a hyper-productive performance state, at will. It might even have been something to do with the 20 hours being tattooed as part of my pain management training! Or it might simply have been the determination to get to the other side of what was quite clearly a colossal midlife crisis!

Difficult to say which played a bigger role. One thing I know is I wasn't doing any of the above two and a half years earlier when I couldn't even run for a train without triggering a coughing fit or causing one or other of my knees to lock up. By accident or by design, all of the preceding factors contributed to my individual version of what I'm calling *Unashamedly Superhuman*. My individual version. The important question is: What would yours look like? What will *Unashamedly Superhuman* do for you? Some of the proceeding information may help. Some won't be necessary for you. Reading this book may simply trigger you to discover the perfect performance hacks for you, ones that I've yet to discover.

This book is a manual for success. It assumes that the measure of our success is how much of our potential we have realised. It is important to appreciate that success is not a matter of how well we do in comparison with others. It is how we measure up to the best in ourselves. It's worth mentioning at this point that this book has nothing specifically to do with keeping fit!

It does, however, have everything to do with harnessing your inner power to achieve your greatest professional and personal goals.

Chapter 1

WHAT IS
UNASHAMEDLY
SUPERHUMAN?

Figure 1.1 Who are you?

Unashamedly Superhuman. What it is and what it isn't. . . .

"I'm superhuman!" That's such an unlikely claim. Arrogant? Inaccurate? Deluded!

Although, for sure that wasn't always our viewpoint.

Cast your mind back. Pre-teens most likely. It may have been Marvel comics or Hollywood movies that sparked our imaginations. If I'd asked you then, what would be your superpower of choice, I have a feeling the challenge would have less to do with our belief in whether it's possible and more to do with limiting it to only one!

I've been asking this question of grownups at conferences all over the world.

I'd like to share with you the top five answers from this exhaustive, albeit non peer-reviewed, data.

By the way, before I do, which one would you choose?

Take a second. If you had to pick one superpower, from all the comics, films, and stories that you heard growing up, which would be yours?

Here are the top five answers. . .

At No. 5 we have a tie: **shapeshifting** and **invisibility**.

How cool would it be to be able to look like anybody in the world? Being able to seamlessly blend into any environment.

We'd be able to infiltrate any situation and align ourselves with whomever we choose. Shapeshifters are dangerous not because they can be anybody. No, they are dangerous because no-one can tell if they are looking at a shapeshifter or not. Excellent!

But if shapeshifting isn't the way that you want to escape from the world around you, then perhaps invisibility is more your style? The invisibility trait is one as old as superheroes. Disappearing from plain sight has a myriad of advantages Over the years, invisibility has allowed the heroes to do more than turn invisible. Some have perfected their power so much so that they can create invisible force fields and turn the objects around them invisible, including whole universes. OK. Now it's just getting ridiculous!

One for the politicians at No. 4: **mind control**. Controversial?

Imagine how much power you could attain if you could control the minds of everyone around you. Like many of the other superpowers, mind control is incredibly old. Maybe mind control, whether controlling others or even our own is the best of the traditional superhero powers. If you don't agree with me, remember this. It doesn't matter which superpower you have. If you have no control over what you're doing, the power is useless. Just a thought.

No. 3 is a surprise entry: **elemental control**. What is that?

If living in the United Kingdom has taught me anything it's this: If you don't like the weather, give it a day or two, it'll change. Four seasons in one day isn't just a catchy Crowded House tune, it's a regular forecast in my hometown back in Wales. Waiting for the weather to change is one thing, but being able to change the weather when you want to is another. My personal favourite.

In the runner's-up spot is **superhuman strength**.

Wouldn't it be amazing to be able to pick up a car and throw it the length of a football field? Although I can't think of too many instances where this would be useful, just being able to do it would be awesome. Super strength is one of the most basic traditional superhero powers. From the early days of comics, most heroes typically came with it. Superman, Thor, Captain America, and Wonder Woman. The reasoning is simple. When heroes are stronger than any who oppose them, it makes victory a near certainty.

Finally, No. 1 on the superpower of choice list, consistently, is **the ability to fly**.

Of all the traditional superhero powers, very few are as common as flight. Flight and superheroes go hand in hand. I suspect it has something to do with safety as much as it does excitement. Whether on an overly bumpy holiday flight or when running late for a date, surely at some point in life everyone has had the thought, I wish I could fly.

I want to make it clear that *Unashamedly Superhuman* has nothing to do with wishing for an impossible, miraculous, and freakish ability.

So what is it then? Let's start with the word *superhuman*. Wikipedia defines it like this:

The term superhuman *refers to enhanced qualities and abilities not naturally found in humans. These qualities can be acquired through a unique ability, technological aids or by self-actualisation.*

Let's take a closer look. . . .

The term superhuman refers to enhanced qualities and abilities that exceed those naturally *found in humans.* So it's already suggesting it's unnatural and different from the rest of us normal people. We tend to save that label superhuman for those rare few, those individuals who have achieved something miraculous. The seemingly impossible. They're not like us.

It goes on to say, "*these qualities may be acquired,* (excellent news), *through a unique ability* (which I've already ruled out), or *by technological aids.*" That's an interesting one, technological aids. I suppose that's the one we've all taken advantage of in order to give ourselves an edge.

We walk around with our phones practically strapped to our hand, which gives us a tremendous amount of additional capability. Complex mathematical calculations resolved in seconds. Every book ever written at our fingertips. Any question asked, answered anytime, anywhere, immediately.

Recently I've taken advantage of a plastic contraption that looks like a low budget bionic arm. Coco, my Jackapoo is blown away by my new-found super-owner ability to launch her tennis ball 10 times farther than other owners. You may have come across this contraption yourself. Coco's not the only one who's happy. I'm delighted too as it delivers a significant performance improvement yet requires zero extra effort, which perhaps sums up the appeal of acquiring any superpower.

Which brings us onto the last of the three options offered by Wikipedia. It concluded, *Superhuman can be achieved through self-actualisation.* Self-actualisation? What even is that? Sounds about as unattainable as waking up with the ability to shape-shift.

Put simply, self-actualisation is the realisation of our full potential. Now, I don't know what you think about that over simplified statement.

For me, whenever I've heard motivational speakers or well-meaning managers announce that in order for me to achieve the results I want I simply need to tap into my potential, my inner critic would wake up and laugh loudly, and continue to do so until such time as I pulled myself together and got on with something more practical. While we're at it, talking about motivational speakers, let me also reassure you, my intention here isn't to try to motivate you. I'm sure that you, like me, have been to many meetings and conferences where they introduce the guest speaker, "Please make some noise for our speaker for today who has flown in especially to motivate you."

At which point you sit back, fold your arms tightly, and frown. Your eyebrows drop and just one side of your mouth rises. The accompanying thought goes something like: Oh, really. Well just you try, Hank! An hour later Hank's crawling off stage. You raise your arms and declare triumphantly, "I'm still de-motivated!" Or perhaps that's just me.

My point being, the term *tapping our full potential* sounds motivational but it provides us with nothing specific that would enable us to actually do so. It's too abstract to be of any practical use. And yet it makes sense intuitively.

Consider this: How much of your potential do you feel you're currently tapping into? If you had to put a number on it out of 100 percent, what feels about right for you right now? Not in any specific area, just generally, in life?

I've been asking this question a lot lately on webinars. Surprisingly, the numbers come into the chat box thick and fast. 60 percent, 75 percent, 20 percent. I say surprisingly because when you think about it it's quite an achievement actually coming up with a number. It's a complex process. Cross-referencing everything you've achieved in the past with everything you believe is possible in the future in around five seconds.

What is less surprising but essentially the point of me asking the question is that nobody ever types in 100 percent. Not one. Never. No one is sitting there thinking, "I'm tapping all of it, Jim," or "I've got nothing left."

It's this faith in possibility, this feeling of certainty that we have access to something more that triggered a conversation resulting in *Unashamedly Superhuman*.

I'd spoken at an event in the United Kingdom for one of the big four accountancy firms. I was talking to my client afterwards who had recently been promoted into a senior role leading a large global team, and she asked if I had any training programmes that would marry together two specific outcomes. High performance AND well-being.

It sounded like an oxymoron. Can you have both? Can you push yourself to your limits and at the same time truly look after yourself?

It wasn't long ago when burnout was considered a badge of honour. It was almost an acceptable price to pay for success. First in and last out was the desirable brand, if you wanted to get ahead. Finally, we're coming around to the view that it's not only ineffective, it's unacceptable. People get hurt. I heard recently that Kevin Johnson, CEO of Starbucks, announced that mental health support is now considered an employee benefit, and many other organisations are blazing a similar trail. However, there's an unavoidable caveat. And that is that many of the things that cause the stress and the pressure haven't gone anywhere. Things aren't getting any easier. The bar of expectation continues to rise. Competition is fierce. Growth targets always point north. In some companies it is still very much a case of up or out. So what's the solution?

I accepted the challenge to find strategies that actually ticked both boxes. Strategies that could genuinely help people to drive productivity to new levels of achievement, whilst at the same time factoring in longevity and sustainability.

The resulting principles, ideas, and techniques are equally for people who are pushing themselves towards the edge of their capability and looking to achieve extraordinary results and for those that are happy to continue achieving exactly the same results but they'd like to have more energy left in the tank at the end of their day. They'd like to give their family their best, not just what's left.

So, the challenge was high performance and well-being. Not one or the other, but both. I was excited and most certainly challenged. Excited because I believed it would provide solutions to the age-old conundrum of establishing and fulfilling a successful work-life balance and challenged because I genuinely had no idea where to start.

I'd spent 25 years focusing on the principles, ideas, and techniques that lent themselves to driving performance. At the time *well-being* was not a word often seen on the company values.

Of course, the topic of well-being is nothing new. It's been debated since the 3rd century BC. The philosopher Aristotle came up with the concept of Eudaimonia – the contented state of feeling healthy, happy, and prosperous. Bringing it right up to date, *The Oxford English Dictionary* defines it as a state of being comfortable, healthy, or happy. Sounds great except I've never met a high-flying, Type A corporate exec who accredited his or her success to any of the previous traits.

The fact is, in life we have to prioritise our time and select the activities that lead us to our most important goals. In pursuit of these there are *must do* activities, *should do* activities, and then at the bottom of the hierarchy of importance you have the *nice to do* activities. The companies that I'd worked for set their priorities in order to drive a high-performance culture. One that gets results. The oft-used phrase in the boardroom goes something like: "There is no mission without margin."

Frankly, looking after yourself was never promoted as a must. For all the spin in the company branding, in reality it languished somewhere between should do and nice to do.

For this to work in my world I would have to approach this from an angle that continued to celebrate essential elements like graft, grit, and resilience as well as promoting the tangible benefits of operating outside the comfort zone, in or out of the box and doing whatever it takes to go the extra mile. In addition, I would have to brand well-being as a means to provide the high octane fuel that can drive you to new and extraordinary levels of achievement.

All I needed to do now was prove that this was true too. And what better way to prove this works than to feel it for myself.

That'll be where the triathlon came in. . . .

For a year I didn't mention it to anyone outside a small circle of friends and family. Even then the response I got was typically *what* followed by *why*? Both fair.

It had to be ridiculous. A challenge so outrageous that it would require a completely new set of strategies. New knowledge, new skills, new processes, and most certainly new mindsets and beliefs. If I were to gain a true understanding of how to combine high performance and well-being, I had to test the ideas for myself.

The business world has a phrase for such objectives: BHAGs (Big Hairy Audacious Goals). On the cover of this book is a bold statement: "harness your inner power and achieve your greatest professional and personal goals." The content for this book was created whilst I was in the process of achieving one of mine. It's worth mentioning that I decided any idea that made it into the book would have to be pushed through three filters. First, in

WHAT IS UNASHAMEDLY SUPERHUMAN? / 13

order to look you in the eye it was important for me to test them. Hence the unlikely self-imposed challenge that I'll mention shortly. Second, each performance hack had to be grounded in neuroscience. We're different in many ways, background, upbringing, education, life experiences, to name a few, but one thing we all share is a central nervous system. Our brain and the operating systems that drive our thoughts, feelings, and patterns of behaviour are essentially the same. I wanted to find tried and tested techniques that didn't just work for me, but worked for everyone. Every time. Finally they also had to have applications in the real world. In other words not everyone is interested in the science; they just want to get results. Can these techniques be applied in the pursuit of business objectives?

Even ridiculous ones like an IRONMAN® triathlon, my personal BHAG.

So, why take on an extreme test of endurance for a book that connects to business performance? It's important at this stage that I give some context.

There will be readers who have taken on significant feats of endurance and yet in spite of their achievement deemed them not necessarily book-worthy. Fair enough. So why do I? First, it provided a perfect set of circumstances for me to cross reference everything I learned from my research, and the results were immediate and undeniable. It also provided a metaphor to hang the learning points on.

What made it a BHAG?

First, I wasn't a triathlete, let alone an IRONMAN® triathlete. The fact is, I wasn't even an athlete. I had done a couple of marathons (1984 in Cardiff, and most recently the year 2000 when I joined a group of colleagues for a charity run in London). Not recent enough to provide any helpful associations, particularly considering the numerous surgeries that soon followed.

It turned out I wasn't built for running. Two six-inch titanium rods screwed either side of my spine to facilitate a double disc fusion and three subsequent knee surgeries would suggest that was the case. My surgeon suggested I limit my exercise to walking, swimming, or *have you considered table tennis?*

Following my run of surgeries I took the doctor's advice to ease back on pounding the pavements and instead substituted exercise for an enthusiasm for fine wines and Marlborough Lights. Good for the knees, not good for much else.

I'm trying to paint a picture that contextualises where I was physically in May 2018, when I decided to take on this physical challenge. The photo at the top of the book probably did the trick. Large glass of red, cigarette, breasts. Nothing inherently wrong with any of that, but not ideal given that in August 2019 I'd signed up to be on the start line in Denmark with 1,500 others for IRONMAN® Copenhagen. When I say physical challenge, the thought of a 3.8-km (2.4-m) swim followed by a 180-km (112-m) bike ride and then a 42.2-km (26.2-m) run was equally daunting psychologically. IRONMAN® triathlons are not for fun-runners. It was a serious event for serious athletes. I couldn't claim to be that, but I certainly could claim to be serious about my objective of meeting my client's challenge of how can you genuinely combine high performance and well-being. For me to do that I would have to complete the IRONMAN® race and feel better at the end of the event day than I did at the beginning. In fact, not just feel better; I would have to feel stronger. No surgeries, no injuries.

As far as I was concerned I might as well have been asking for some comic book level superpower. . . .

What was supposed to be a 12-month BHAG designed to help me test a few developmental theories turned out to be a two-and-a-half-year adventure that involved ambulances, hospitalisation, cancellations, and a global pandemic. We get to all that later in this book.

As the saying goes, all's well that ends well. Job done on a cold September in Reading of all places. I couldn't have enjoyed the day more; however, without doubt the true value of the experience wasn't completing the distance; it was about everything that I'd learned and become during the two-and-a-half-year adventure.

Chapter 2

SUPERHERO ORIGIN STORIES

"Why is every superhero movie an origin story?" Perhaps we love origin stories because they "show the exact moment when a normal person goes from being just like us to being somehow better, smarter, or stronger."

It seems that superheroes undergo three types of life-altering experiences that we can relate to and draw inspiration from.

The first is trauma, which lies at the heart of Batman's origin story, in which Bruce Wayne dedicates himself to fighting crime after seeing his parents murdered. In real life, many people experience "stress-induced growth" after a trauma and resolve to help others, even becoming social activists.

The second life-altering force is destiny. Consider *Buffy the Vampire Slayer* about a normal teenager who discovers she's the "Chosen One"—endowed with supernatural powers to fight demons. Buffy is reluctant to accept her destiny, yet she throws herself into her new job. Many of us identify with Buffy's challenge, minus the vampires, of assuming a great responsibility that compels her to grow up sooner than she wants to.

Last, there's sheer chance, which transformed a young Spider-Man, who was using his power for selfish purposes until his beloved uncle was murdered by a street thug. Spider-Man's heroism is an example of how random adverse events cause many of us to take stock of our lives and choose a different path.

At their best, superhero origin stories inspire us and provide models of coping with adversity, finding meaning in loss and trauma, discovering our strengths, and using them for good purpose. Wearing a cape or tights is optional.

If there is a pattern and some common traits that often occur where the ordinary person becomes *super* it's that their powers appear randomly, under stress and, initially at least, appear out of control. Think the Incredible Hulk.

Of course, it would be easy to write off all of these superhuman capabilities as mere fantasy and ones that reside only in the world of the supernatural, but maybe super *natural* would be an equally valid concept.

I was in the United States some years ago, and this story came on the news. I always thought the stories of how people summon up superhuman strength to lift their car off their child or grand-child were just urban myths or newsworthy attention seekers. Yet here was a lady being interviewed in front of me on the local news bulletin. The interviewer said, "You lifted the car off your son. You found some superhuman capability. An incredible achievement, how did you do it?" What was most interesting was the reluctance of the hero of the hour to talk about it. She was quite dismissive, angry even. She huffed and puffed whilst expressing the relief she felt at preventing any serious injury to her young son, but when it came to taking any glory she rapidly lost interest. The news anchor pressed on, "You don't seem too happy to have achieved what most would regard as miraculous." Her reply was fascinating, "Why couldn't it have happened 20 years ago?" "What do you mean," he asked.

"I wish I'd known I could do that when I was younger. It's no use to me now!" she said. She was less impressed by what she had suddenly learned about her capabilities and more distressed about how her life could have been had she known growing up that she had this dormant inner strength. It's a fair point, don't you think?

Neither the journalist, nor the Super Lady in question, was able to explain what happened that day, *Unashamedly Superhuman* will shed some light.

Let me distil everything in this book down into a single statement:

Combining high performance and well-being is a func-tion of the skillful management and mobilisation of our energy. Furthermore, we all have an in-built set of resources that, when harnessed and deployed, can immediately elevate our performance to a superhuman level.

It's a big claim. Bench pressing sports cars aside I am saying that every performance hack and well-being principle we look at, if applied with a modicum of enthusiasm, will have a direct impact on the emotional state you experience, and your ability to gain access to your full cognitive and physiological capability.

I considered putting *if applied* in capital letters, but then thought no. Not necessary. When you picked up this book and thought, "Superhuman? That could come in handy," you didn't expect the solution would be a random happening or the combination of a wand and the magic word *abracadabra*. No, even if the claim of superhuman status was met with an appropriate amount of scepticism, you would fully expect to be personally involved in the developmental process. You'd expect to have to take some action and run your own experiment.

So with that in mind, before we go any further, I want to give you an opportunity to prove to yourself that right now, as you sit reading, there exists a remarkable, in-built system waiting for you to tap into and reveal superhuman capability.

Superhuman isn't just something you have to work at, it's also something you already are. It's in-built, and here's how we're going to prove it.

I'd like to invite you to use the QR code on page 20 and come and join me in a demonstration that will blow your mind, in a good way.

This is the perfect metaphor for what it means to be *Unashamedly Superhuman.*

You will tap into a readily available resource and see an immediate and dramatic improvement in your performance. You will literally tap into your potential. Rather than just understand this hack you will experience it and feel its benefits.

Let's start by establishing a benchmark. You need a stopwatch for this.

I appreciate that it's unusual to stop while you're reading to test an idea, literally in the moment, but frankly this is an unusual book. The focus is not just on understanding the hacks that connect performance and well-being, it's about doing them, testing them, and letting your results be the judge. So, in this breath-holding exercise, just breathe out and at the end of your exhale with empty lungs, pause, hold your breath and start the clock. Hold your breath and start the clock. No force, no effort, no turning blue. As soon as you feel the urge to breathe back in, do so, and make a note of the time. It's not a competition. Longer isn't better than shorter. It's just a benchmark. How long can you hold your breath after the exhale, on empty lungs? OK. We'll come back to that.

Check out the following simple instructions or click on the QR and join me. We're going to repeat the process three times. The first one is practice, the second one is getting familiar, and the third one is the real deal.

The Exercise

Part one

Sit comfortably or lie down.
Take in 30 full, deep breaths. Fully in then let go. Fully in then let go. No gap between exhale and inhale. Make it circular. Feeling light-headed or tingling sensations are normal. Keep going, fully in and let go. About the same effort level as a fast walk. We're looking for focused but not forced. After the 30th breath, you breathe out and STOP.
Don't breathe back in, just relax and hold.

Part two

Wait calmly until you feel the need to breathe back in. You may surprise yourself with how long you can comfortably pause. When you do feel the urge to breathe back in, take one full recovery breath (stop the stopwatch) hold your breath for the count of 15, and enjoy!

Some FAQs

Should I breathe in through my mouth or nose?
Whichever is more comfortable. Mix it up a bit. The objective is simply to take in full breaths.
Can I do this whilst on the move?
Nope. Sitting or lying down only. The more comfortable you are the better the result. As you over-oxygenate, it's normal to experience light-headedness. Enjoyable when you're sitting comfortably, not particularly helpful when driving or operating heavy machinery.

> *Does it have to be exactly 30 breaths?*
> No, although 30 to 35 seems to be an optimal number.
> *Should I breathe fast or slow?*
> Faster is more energising whilst slower is more relaxing. I'd suggest steady, full inhales for the count of two or three. When you exhale, you don't need to fully exhale, just let it fall out, nice and easy.
> OK, let's do it!
> For maximum effect, I would encourage three rounds. The first round is to get used to it.
> The second round is to practice relaxing into the process, and then the third round is for real!
> Time the breath hold on the third round. Enjoy.
> *Note*: This exercise is not advised if you're pregnant or if you have any pulmonary conditions.

As I mentioned, we review in the next sections of the book the numerous benefits of this respiratory protocol and how it can be used as a priming exercise before any activity that requires energy, composure, and focus. But for now it's just to provide some data. How long did you effortlessly hold your breath with no oxygen in your lungs after the third round? I wouldn't be surprised if after three rounds of this simple respiratory protocol you effortlessly held your breath for two minutes or more.

It would be an outrageous claim if you hadn't just had the experience and proven it for yourself. (If you're still reading and you didn't actually do it, now is a good time to scan the QR code and join me.) Seeing is believing!

If this only demonstrates one thing, that there is more to you than meets the eye, then at this stage that is mission accomplished. As we work through the content of *Unashamedly Superhuman* there will be many more demonstrations of how to tap into readily available resources that will enable you to do a whole range of things from reducing stress levels to creating a boost in energy. From generating extreme levels of focus and clarity to triggering motivation and momentum. From carving out goals and aspirations that tap into purpose and meaning to developing the personal strengths that combine passion, competence, and organisational needs.

Although the more attractive word in this book's title is *Superhuman*, the more important word is undoubtedly *Unashamedly*.

So, before we launch into how we're going to unleash our full potential my final question to you is this: What will you do with your new-found inner Superhuman?

It seems that after the random event that suddenly revealed their new-found ability, superhumans tended to have a tremendous focus that caused the likes of Peter Parker to hone their skills and direct them towards something meaningful.

This book is designed to support you in turning your personal BHAGs into reality.

BETTER – TAPPING INTO POTENTIAL

"Tapping into your potential" is a phrase you've probably heard many times before, but what does it mean and how does it connect to Better? In many ways, it's simple mathematics. If I'm only using 60 percent of my potential right now, and I tap into some of the remaining 40 percent, it's sure to mean an uplift in output. Whether it's gaining access to specific skill sets or more abstract attitudes and emotions, the additional capacity will no doubt enable us to both respond better to our challenges and perform better in the moments that matter.

Why start here though? Without tapping into your potential, you can't unlock the superhuman within. Potential is where your superhuman resides and when you can access that at will, you have the ability to improve your performance in any area of life.

Throughout the chapters in this part of the book, I share a series of performance hacks that will help you tap into unutilised potential and set you on your own path towards becoming *Unashamedly Superhuman.*

Let's start in Chapter 3 by exploring exactly what *potential* means and, more importantly, how you can tap into it reliably and consistently, whenever you need to.

It's time to fly.

TAPPING INTO POTENTIAL

One of the things that enable us to keep moving forward in the most demanding of conditions is the ability to adapt more in order to endure less *Potential*. What is it? *The Oxford English Dictionary* defines it as:

Potential generally refers to a currently unrealized ability. The term is used in a wide variety of fields, from physics to the social sciences, to indicate things that are in a state where they are able to change in ways ranging from the simple release of energy by objects to the realisation of abilities in people.

Try this. Just take your arm and lift it up as high as you can. Point your index finger into the air and push it as high as you can. That's it. Now look at how high you can lift it up. For the sake of the demonstration let's call that your best performance. Your highest. Hold it there for a moment and watch what happens when I now direct you to lift it a bit higher. Ready? GO! That's it, raise your arm higher. Excellent!

Here's the question. Where did that extra bit come from? You'd lifted it as high as you could: "That's my highest, Jim." "That's my best." And then I asked you to raise it a bit more." You may say, "What, that bit?! But that bit represents potential. It was always there. Always available, but something had to happen before it revealed itself.

The objective of Chapter 3 is to take what can be a vague and somewhat abstract concept of tapping potential and demystify it to the point where you not only recognise yourself in the description, but you also have a repeatable strategy for its achievement. Let's look at an applied definition, clinically speaking.

When I heard what I'm about to share with you, it transformed the concept of tapping potential from a self-help motivational tool into a pragmatic and precise set of stepping stones.

Jordan B. Peterson is a psychology professor emeritus at the University of Toronto and a clinical psychologist with two main areas of study: the psychology of belief, including religion, mythology, and political ideology; and the assessment and improvement of personality, including the prediction of creativity and academic and industrial performance. He began to receive widespread attention in the late 2010s for his views on cultural and political issues, often described as conservative.

With an active social media presence and a forthright delivery style, I think it's fair to describe Mr Peterson as Marmite®. That aside, his take on what it takes to successfully tap into untapped resources for me is nothing short of inspired. See what you think.

He starts by saying that we already know from a clinical perspective that we need to set out a path towards a goal, the reason being that an aspiration triggers a positive emotion. It would seem that by choosing a goal it implies a hierarchy in terms of how we make decisions.

You decide that you're going to prioritise your goal over and above other things. Applying your focus and energy in the direction of a specific goal typically results in you experiencing a positive emotion as you watch yourself move towards your goal.

The more important the goal, the more enriched your experience. He talks about the value of not just developing a vision but aiming at the highest goal that you can manage.

If it genuinely stretches you and takes you outside your comfort zone, what you'll find is that as you move towards the goal, there are certain things that you have to accomplish that frighten you. Maybe you have to learn to be a better communicator, a better manager, a better thinker. You have to be better to people around you, or you have to learn some new skills. However, doing something new is not only challenging, it also provides new information. Then we can incorporate that information and turn it into a new skill. So far so good.

Then it gets really interesting. He started diving into genetic codes.

He said if you put yourself into a new situation, new gene codes and new neural structures are formed. For example, imagine you're working out. You push against heavy resistance. Your muscles are responding to the load. It's the same with your nervous system.

Imagine there's potential locked into your genetic code. You then put yourself in a new situation and it turns out the situational stress unlocks those genes and then builds new parts of you. So the question is: How much potential is locked inside of you?

Well, let's assume that scale's-up. You take on heavier and heavier loads. You get more informed because you're doing more difficult things and, as a result, more of you gets unlocked. The more we take on, the more we gain access to what's available to us?

Professor Peterson goes on to say that all of our ancestral wisdom is locked inside of us, biologically. And the bigger the challenge, the more that's going to tap into the reserves of potential waiting to be hacked. I'm going to leave the final line to JP.

"As you push yourself harder, what you could be clicks into place. You are the consequence of all these living beings that have come before you, and that's all part of your biological potentiality."[1]

Not sure I've seen a more concise explanation for tapping into potential.

I don't believe what Professor Peterson says is designed to be a motivational speech, yet I don't ever remember feeling more motivated. Stretching ourselves and taking on the greatest possible challenge now seemed an obligation with the objective to find out how much is genetically locked inside. My situational stress of choice just happened to be an IRONMAN® triathlon. The notion that everything required for its achievement was already locked inside was without doubt a game-changer. Even though at that point I had no idea how, for the first time in my life I felt I was consciously experiencing what Carol Dweck referred to in her book *Mindset*[2] as a growth mindset and not a fixed one.

[1] Thought Feeder, (2019), *A Powerful Secret to Unlocking Your Potential*, YouTube. Available at: https://www.youtube.com/watch?v=FU1Po6qH7O8.
[2] Dweck, C., (2007), *Mindset: The New Psychology of Success*, Ballantine Books, Reprint edition.

Stepping up

Strangely, in the history of performance psychology the idea that we could significantly improve over time was considered unlikely.

We could learn new technical skills, pick up a musical instrument or develop new business strategies but our ability to add psychological capacities like resilience, focus, or even empathy was believed to be pretty much done by the age of 25.

But a Harvard psychologist named Robert Kegan reversed that belief. He discovered that while some adults remained frozen in time, a few, and it was the minority, did achieve meaningful growth and development.

He defined people in this group as having expanded their ability to do two things: (1) to explore and hold differing viewpoints, and (2) to develop a flexibility in how they thought about themselves. In other words, they were able to define themselves not just based on their past results, but also based on who or what they wanted to become. Nowadays we'd call it having a GROWTH mindset, a fundamental belief that learning and self-development are lifelong pursuits.

Not everyone believes that, and as a result not everyone steps up to another level of capability. The reason I was so inspired to share Prof Peterson's take on how to tap potential was to provide a paradigm for how to shift our mindset from fixed to growth.

I also find his perspective on suffering to be strangely refreshing, in that it is a worthwhile and necessary part of the pursuit of meaningful success. But I believe there's a time and a place for endurance. Developing grit and resilience can be greatly enhanced from controlled exposure to difficult and challenging environments but it can't be the only model. We'll revisit this empowering reframe later in the book, but for now I'd like to introduce a model and a set of performance hacks that are designed to minimise any unnecessary suffering.

How we respond to change in general would be a good example of this. Are we just experiencing situational stress or are we attaching a predetermined goal in order to give the external change some meaning? Injecting a positive meaning to the change creates motive, drive, and positive expectation. The question isn't whether we'll experience highs and lows, the question is can we determine whether we keep moving forward in a productive and resourceful way?

The model in Figure 3.1 highlights an inevitable combination. Two factors that, assuming we have the relevant knowledge and skills for the job at hand, have a decisive impact on whether or not our hard-earned skills "show up" and enable us to achieve our desired outcomes. The X-axis represents the circumstances that we find ourselves in. On the right, the easiest, most comfortable, and favourable situations. To the far left of the model, the most demanding, difficult, and challenging circumstances.

It's important to stress that the top of the Y-axis represents an optimum state of mind, the most useful state of mind given the circumstances. I'm not talking positive at the top and negative at the bottom. It depends. If your desired outcome is to go to sleep,

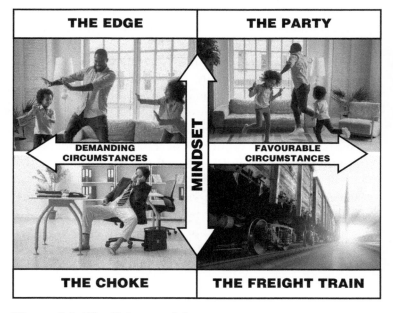

Figure 3.1 The Edge model

"energised" would represent a suboptimal state of mind, that is, not helpful!

Imagine you've taken the opportunity to do a parachute jump. Before take-off, whilst checking the parachute, what would be the optimum state of mind? I would argue that it would be pessimistic or sceptical.

The pessimist never forgets to check everything. How many times? Many times. The pessimist has no problem with those "difficult" conversations: "Who packed this parachute?" "How many have you packed before?" Pessimism is the perfect state of mind for checking parachutes. However, when you are 12,000 feet up (3,658 metres), it's probably best to become an optimist! Nothing to do with being positive or negative, right or wrong, having a good or bad attitude. It would just be a more useful state bearing in mind the change in circumstances.

On the ground, pessimism was perfect; 12,000 feet (3,658 metres) up, it prevents us from doing the one thing we are there to do: Jump! We have the necessary skills to jump, but as the circumstances changed from favourable to demanding what was lacking was control. Control over our mindset. In fact, in this example the circumstances dictated it.

So, as you look at this model I'm sure you'll recognise yourself in the four quadrants. The top right-hand quadrant, The Party, and the bottom left, The Choke, are perhaps the most obvious. The Party is the perfect combination of favourable circumstances with optimum mindsets. Everything is going our way. Clients love us. The market is bullish. We're ahead of our targets. The tail wind is blowing hard. To cap it off, we're feeling calm and confident, on top of the world. It's time to celebrate.

The bottom left, The Choke zone, couldn't be more different. Simply consider the opposite of all of the preceding feelings. Wading through treacle with the world on our shoulders. It's not necessarily that we lack the ability to get the job done, it's more that we lack access to our abilities. A sporting analogy may help. You're on the driving range loosening up before a big game. No pressure. Hitting practice balls one after another straight down the middle of the range. Then you head to the first tee. There's a crowd watching and money riding on it. Suddenly it's like you're a completely different human being. You can't feel your hands let alone the golf club. Or you've prepared your presentation, got all your slides in order, and you just need to deliver it to secure the game-changing contract, and then they hand you the clicker and you get as far as "Good morning my name is. . . ." and then nothing. Blank!

Psychologists call it discombobulated (the funniest word to describe a most unfunny state of mind). What I'm talking about is extremely demanding circumstances coupled with suboptimal emotional states. Perhaps fear of failure would reside here, perhaps stressed out, overwhelm for sure.

If you're human you will have experienced the top right and the bottom left-hand quadrants more than once. The bottom right is an interesting one. I use the image of a freight train here as it connects to the phrase, the freight train's coming! If there is one word that sums up the bottom right-hand quadrant it would be *complacency*. However, in the bottom right-hand quadrant our lack of resourcefulness is, temporarily at least, less problematic because we're being propped up by the supportive circumstances. Imagine if you were selling property in 2006–2007. For the most part it was a seller's market. You could have been an underwhelming real estate agent who didn't bounce into work in the morning with a spring in your step. That's not a problem as property is still flying off the shelf, in spite of you. Which is fine, so long as what doesn't change? That's right, the circumstances. The market. Unfortunately it did. Dramatically. In that moment the journey from bottom right to bottom left is rapid and disorientating. Discombobulating. Not funny. So, we have a choice: Wait until the circumstances shift us back to the right-hand side of the model or have a strategy to elevate us to the top left-hand quadrant. The Edge.

Having facilitated many teams through this model with a view to establishing their current circumstances and establishing a route to their desired circumstances, far and away the most consistent insight that I've taken away is this: Without exception, the quadrant that high performers gravitate towards is top left and not top right. It's where it's at!

But, why? Why would you prefer to be there? Maybe it's the challenge. Some people just like a challenge. Perhaps it has something to do with the sense of achievement. A hard-earned victory is infinitely more rewarding than an easy win. Of course, the trade-off for the effort required to compete in the top left could be the education you receive. The growth curve is constant. And then, of course, there is the confidence and the resilience; two resources that are forged in adversity.

Mihaly Csikszentmihalyi, Hungarian-American psychologist and author of *Flow: The Psychology of Optimal Experience*,[3] puts it like this, "The best moments in our life are not the passive, relaxing times. The best moments usually occur if a person's body and mind is stretched to its limits in a voluntary effort to accomplish something difficult and worthwhile."

Until the summer of 2020 I'd never heard of the term *VUCA world*. Since then it seems to have become part of every leadership consultants tool kit. VUCA is an acronym, first used in 1987 and based on the leadership theories of Warren Bennis and Burt Nanus,[4] that stands for Volatility, Uncertainty, Complexity, and Ambiguity. It was the response of the US Army War College to the collapse of the USSR in the early 1990s.

During our lifetimes we've all had to manage circumstances where one or two of the preceding have challenged us and tested our resources: mental, physical, and possibly spiritual for those who believe. For a situation to arise where all four collide at the same time at the same place for everyone was, to say the least, unusual.

[3] Csikszentmihalyi, M., (2008), *Flow: The Psychology of Optimal Experience*, Ingram International Inc.
[4] Bennis, W. and Nanus, B., (1987), "Leaders: The Strategies for Taking Charge," New York: Harper and Row, 1985. *NASSP Bulletin*, 171(500): 130–130. doi:10.1177/019263658707150021.

To survive and thrive in a VUCA world, we need Vision, Understanding, Clarity, and Agility – the counterweight to Volatility, Uncertainty, Complexity, and Ambiguity. Developing these four capabilities is essential if we are to survive in a VUCA world. The principles, ideas, and techniques in *Unashamedly Superhuman* enable us to "ride the rapids." In a VUCA world, we are always in command of our response, even if we're not necessarily in control of our environment.

Chapter 4

ACCEPT THE ADVENTURE

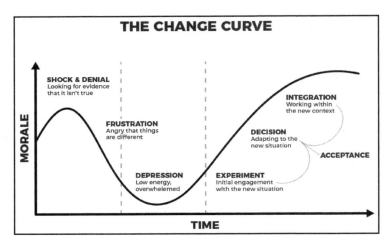

Figure 4.1 Kübler-Ross Change Curve®

The change challenge

There can't have been many periods in our lives where everyone we know was embarking on a journey through the Kübler-Ross Change Curve®[1] (Figure 4.1) at exactly the same time. However, from March 2020 it appeared that the vast majority of the people found themselves, to one degree or another, at the top of this model. (I agree the pandemic isn't the only challenge in town, but it's probably worth a mention even if it's worded specifically as a metaphor.)

Although the psychological journey from shock and denial to integration seems logical, the difference, from person to person, in the quality of the experience and the time it took to reverse the trajectory of the change curve varied dramatically. There are many reasons to explain that. But instead of diving down that rabbit hole, I want to focus the discussion specifically on the turning point. How did you turn it around? How did you adapt? At the heart of the survival of the fittest theory is the

---

[1]Kübler-Ross, E., (2008), *On Death and Dying*, Routledge, 40th anniversary illustrated edition.

ability to ADAPT. Darwin says that is isn't the strongest species that thrive, it is the ones that adapt the best to changing environments, *The Origin of Species.*[2]

When reflecting on Prof Peterson's academic take on how to tap potential and on how we successfully adapted to the wide range of behavioural changes that were brought about in 2020, there seems to be a repeatable pattern of five specific elements.

The first of which is also the fundamental turning point on the Kubler-Ross change curve, that point where we pull out of the downward trajectory and start to turn things around for the better. Step one is *Accept.*

Performance = Potential − Interference

More often than not, this is the first model I introduce when working with teams looking to break through the barriers that are impeding their performance. It's a simple concept. Our performance is a reflection of how good we could be minus the things that are getting in our way. Although it's a simple concept, it often unveils a series of complex challenges to overcome. First off, we have to agree that we do at least have some potential available to tap into. It's an important admission and an empowering realisation to accept that there is indeed more to be had. This is even more powerful when we take time to explore the important question, what are all the interferences that are currently getting in the way? This is made even more powerful when we follow that up by removing them from our business or, if we're applying the model to ourselves, our lives. We'll get to that, but for now focus your attention on the friction that is slowing up your progress.

Interference is anything that could possibly have a negative impact on our performance. The answers can be many and varied and are, of course, specific to us. Take out a piece of paper

[2]Darwin, C., (2011), *The Origin of Species (Collins Classics),* William Collins, UK edition.

and just go for it; write down all the interferences you can think of. Don't try to make sense of the list, just create one. It doesn't matter what it is, just be honest and momentarily suspend any thoughts as to why it is, how it happened, who is involved and who's at fault. If it comes to mind, write it down. For example. . .

- Difficult market conditions
- Rising inflation
- Competitive competition
- Fatigue
- Boredom
- Stress
- Lack of support
- Difficult people
- Lack of motivation
- Global pandemics
- Way too many distractions
- Too much to do and no time to do it
- Unorganised
- Uninspired
- The weather
- Feeling under the weather and underwhelmed

Get the idea? It sounds like the mother of all negative brainstorms. No matter, we haven't finished yet!

Before leaving the scene of your negativity-fest, you must immediately push your list through a couple of filters. First, would you consider each interference on your list to be your doing or is it the result of outside forces? In other words, as you look at each one, I'm inviting you to decide if it being in your life is in any way within your control to remove. This is where the complexity kicks in.

Let's use my list and see. Some will be obvious, for example, difficult market conditions, rising inflation, competitive competition, pandemics, and the weather are clearly outside of our control. They are none of our doing. However, fatigue, boredom, stress, lack of motivation, feeling under the weather and underwhelmed, too many distractions, too much to do and no time to do it, unorganised, and uninspired may be things we can do something about, if we know how. Even a lack of support and difficult people, which on the face of it seem outside our control, are probably things we can at least influence if we decided to dedicate our time to them. It depends how sick and tired we are of being sick and tired about these interferences getting in the way of our progress.

Let's not argue the toss over the last two, instead let's at least agree on the fact that we can waste a tremendous amount of time and energy fretting over some things that are out of our control and instead focus what little time we have on removing the interferences that we can.

To help with your decisions let me introduce the second filter. You're going to like this one, although maybe not at first. For some this will be jarring, but trust me it is designed to liberate you. Look at each piece of interference and decide where it resides. OK, here we go.

If you can't accept it, affect it; but if you can't affect it, accept it. Let that sink in for a moment while I tell you a story.

I was invited to Hong Kong to facilitate what I was told would be a particularly difficult group of 50 facilities managers. Half of them were internal employees and the other 25 were their external partners. There was a lack of collaboration among them, resulting in poor performance all round. Anyway, I had them go through the P = P − I process and when I announced the punch line, "If you can't accept it, affect it; but if you can't affect, it accept it," one of the disgruntled delegates stood up and said, "That's the most ridiculous thing I've ever heard!" I asked her to elaborate, and she said, "You may have noticed that there were, in fact, only 49 people present and that the person I work with couldn't even be bothered to turn up." She said he was impossible to work with and that she had tried everything but to no avail, what's more I was suggesting that she should accept her unacceptable situation. The details of their dysfunctional relationship weren't clear, but her frustration was, for all to see. Maybe you can relate.

I empathised and said clearly the situation was unacceptable to her. She agreed. So, I said, if you can't accept it, what are you going to do about it? She repeated, "I've tried everything, there is nothing else I can do." I agreed and said in which case just accept it, to which she spat, "Why should I?! His behaviour is unacceptable." To which I agreed. "If you can't accept it, what are you going to do to affect it?" I repeated. "I just told you," she reminded me, "I've tried everything, I can't affect it." To which again I agreed. "So, if you can't affect it, just accept it," I said again. It didn't land well. We repeated this loop twice more. I stressed that it wasn't my intention to infuriate her, although it seemed I was failing. I reassured her that my intention was simply to help her to break free from a situation where she felt she could neither affect nor accept the interference that was preventing a way forward. I said, "You have to decide one way or the other, affect or accept. If you don't, the consequence is you will just get hotter and hotter." At this point, somebody in the audience interjected, "I know who you are talking about; he is difficult." I immediately asked him, what would you do if he was in her position? Whilst he thought about it I asked the entire room, what have any of you ever done to navigate your way through such a difficult interpersonal situation?

The suggestions came in thick and fast. I asked her to write them down. Within five minutes she had a list of 10 or more. Some she'd already tried, whilst some were new options to her. This was an emotive situation to navigate and although I said that I agreed that it wasn't necessarily her responsibility to fix her challenging relationship, the fact remained that he was her declared interference and therefore the only resourceful way forward was to decide to either affect it or accept it. She chose the former. She contacted me a week or so later to say that she had indeed done just that. They were never going to be buddies, but she had provoked a conversation with him where they had established and resolved their very own

$$P = P - I.$$

Aside from being a useful model when filtering your interferences and prioritising where to focus your attention, how does this connect to the title of this chapter, "Accept the Adventure"?

Well, having accepted the challenge in front of you, you're then in a position to free up your thinking and direct your focus on the next desired state that you want to manifest. You will have prioritised your thinking and started to carve out a vision of the future that energises you and lifts your spirits. You cut through the fog of uncertainty by clarifying what it is you want rather than dwelling on the things that you don't. Adapting, like any behavioural change, takes time and effort. The reason the goal is so vital is that, as the Professor said earlier, it exposes the gap between where we are and where we're trying to get to, causing us to *Activate* new parts of ourselves and develop new capabilities.

Activate is step three. The goal also provides the drive required to keep us moving forward whilst we're endeavouring to adjust our behavioural habits and disciplines. This additional motivation helps us to *Persist*, step four, and bed-in the new behaviours. Finally, step five, *Tune in & Tune up* helps us to keep our focus on both our progress and our continued self-development. You have to tune in and work out what's working for you as well as what isn't. Celebrate your daily and weekly successes and establish the areas for ongoing improvement.

Adapt more/Endure less

Ice is ice. Whichever way you cut-it, it's cold. Very cold. It's 0°C (32°F) at best! No matter where we are, if we're submerged in an ice bath up to our neck, we can safely assume we're experiencing pretty much the exact same conditions. But, of course, just because we're in the same situation doesn't mean we're having the same experience does it? The two images in Figure 4.2 provide an excellent example of both the point and the solutions that we'll be exploring here.

How would you describe the experience of the individual in the image on the left. It looks like an endurance test. I don't

Figure 4.2 Enduring or adapting?

care how tough you are there is only so much you can take. The issue isn't one of commitment and application. Willingness to endure is admirable but is it sustainable?

Look at the next image. What is she doing that he isn't? They're both experiencing the same external circumstances. The young woman in the picture isn't putting up with it. She is getting *from* the challenge not getting *through* it. That is an adaptive mindset. She's found a way to adapt to the circumstances whilst he hasn't. He's having to use up a tremendous amount of his resources in order to cope with the challenge provided by the ice bath. Both endurance and adaptation have a part to play in how we navigate life's challenges and opportunities, but the question here is: Which one is more sustainable?

With my personal challenge of completing the IRONMAN® triathlon, I'd accepted the inevitability that it would be a test of my endurance, but how much would I need to endure, and would it be possible to mitigate some of the suffering by becoming better at adapting more effectively to the demands of the event? Think of it as hydraulic. If you hadn't adapted to all that life has thrown at you, without a doubt it would have been an unbearable test of your endurance. Only by adapting more are we able to endure less.

Performance hack: Conscious cognitive reframe

I read recently that one of the fastest-growing sports over the last 10 years are action adventure sports. Perhaps you have participated in events like Tough Mudder or The Wolf Run or maybe you've also taken on a triathlon or the like.

Why do we call them adventure activities? What words come to mind when you focus on an adventure? What specifically do you associate with being on an adventure? *Challenge* perhaps. *The unknown. Adrenaline. Risk. Excitement. Danger. Fun. Fear. Unpredictable. Uncomfortable* even.

Some of those are positive words, others not so. An adventure isn't dependent on success or failure. Of course, it's just a play on words, semantics. However, the choice of words we use to describe the situation we're facing can significantly impact how we experience it and how we feel about it. In the same way we can redefine a problem as a challenge, we can also reframe a challenge as being part of our adventure. Later in the book we work through the specifics of which goals you would like to achieve in order to make your adventure worthwhile. For now we're just setting up your DOT (direction of travel), your Adventure.

Chapter 5

DIRECT THE SEEKING SYSTEM

At a national sales conference in the UK recently I interviewed Phil Jones MBE, the UK MD of the technology solutions company Brother. I asked for a key lesson that has helped him and his team to adapt to a VUCA world, particularly whilst experiencing a lack of vision and clarity about the future. His answer was inspired and inspiring to all in the audience.

He said, "Don't try too hard to prescribe your future in too much detail." He revealed that at his company, "We work on a philosophy called your DOT. Your dot on the horizon. Your direction of travel." He told us that his was "To be a master of subject matter and achieve mastery of self." He said, "I'm never going to finish that journey of personal growth. That journey never ends. It's a relentless pursuit." He concluded with, "The one thing we must all take as a lesson now is the ability to be more agile. The ability to be more anti-fragile, which is about taking the knocks and not just snapping back to what was after the knock, but taking the knock and building yourself into something new and improved. It's the new you created from the experience."

The reframe "Accept the Adventure" does more than just provoke an upbeat mood as we contemplate the way forward. It also activates a specific part of the brain called the *ventral striatum*. That's the technical term, or we could also call it the *seeking system*. This system is urging us to explore the boundaries of what we know. It's the new and the desire to learn, and we can think about stimulating and activating this part of the brain. For example, when the seeking system is activated, it releases dopamine into our body. Dopamine is a neurotransmitter that makes us feel more alive. Literally, the feeling of zest or enthusiasm or curiosity, wells up within us and it's an innate feeling; it's intrinsic.

That, in turn, immediately influences everything you see in connection to your goal. It's a bit like if you bought a new car, say a grey Audi. What do you start to see everywhere for the next few days? Grey Audis! You're not even looking for them, but they're everywhere. Once the seeking system is switched on, it informs where to focus your attention.

Once you have accepted the adventure and re-focused on your desired direction of travel, an effective way of directing the seeking system still further is to align your vision with the belief in your ability to achieve it. Let me give an example. I was working with a client, and he told me that he had signed up for the London Marathon. He had about five months to go before the run. He told me he was starting to get really stressed by this whole thing. I asked him what he meant. He said, "Well, I read that people have dropped dead during some of these extreme events." I said, "Yeah, I read that as well." He asked, "How am I supposed to deal with that? I'm no athlete. I've got this marathon to do and it's really starting to stress me out. How can I get rid of the stress?"

I told him that if his goal is to reduce the stress, that's easy, just don't do the marathon. Take it out of your schedule and the problem goes away. That's a valid option. If you can change the situation that is causing the stress, then do. Of course, it's not always that easy. He thought about this, then said, "I've got to do it. I've signed up with a charity." I agreed and shared a performance hack to help him. It told him that he had to align his vision with his belief.

I said, "You said a moment ago, 'I'm no athlete.' That's an interesting statement. It's an identity statement. I am no athlete, and you've got a marathon in five months. Do you see a disconnect there? So, from now on if anyone asks you what you do outside of work or what your hobbies and interests are, I want you say, 'I'm a marathon runner'." He looked a little confused and said, "But I haven't done it yet."

I elaborated, "I understand that, but on this occasion you have to tell the truth in advance. Tell the truth early. You're doing the things marathon runners do. You have every right to call yourself a marathon runner! Are you training?" He said, "Yeah, of course." I asked, "How often?" His response was, "Five times a week." I said, "That's what marathon runners do. You're a marathon runner! What else? Have you bought into the

Lycra®? The paper thin lightweight vest and shorts? How about the £200 ($260) shoes? Are you investing in your running?" He said, "Yeah." I said, "And who does that? Marathon runners! You're a marathon runner." Then I dropped the convincer, "I bet you're reading about running too." He said, "Well, I have got a few magazines, *Runner's World* and *220 Triathlon....*" I said, "Who reads about running?" He replied, "Marathon runners?" "Correct!" I replied. "You're doing the things a marathon runner would do, so you can legitimately call yourself a marathon runner."

Here's the main point. Ultimately, I asked, what do marathon runners do? He paused, then replied, "They run marathons." Exactly. They would expect it in their schedule, it wouldn't freak them out. What you're doing by declaring yourself to be a marathon runner is switching on your brain's seeking system to do whatever it has to do to raise your awareness to what it is going to take for you to meet your goal.

Substitute "I am a marathon runner" for "I am a leader" or "I am a manager" or "I am a business owner" or whatever else suits your aspiration. Your definition of you isn't restricted just to your past results. In order to switch on the seeking system it's helpful to factor in the growth required too. Make sense? Sound easy? I thought so until I set the objective to become an IRONMAN® triathlete. If I was taking my own medicine I'd just have to start by saying to myself, "I'm an IRONMAN® competitor." The problem was, I'd never heard anything so bloody ridiculous.

As I mentioned earlier, my motivation was to extract some principles, ideas, and techniques that could legitimately combine high performance and well-being; productivity and sustainability.

I wanted to provoke new ways of thinking, new ways of doing things, tools and techniques that I'd never even heard of before. To stay on theme, I had to tap into my potential and find new parts of myself, whatever that meant. Professor Peterson said, "Set a goal that's ridiculous. One that is so far outside your comfort zone, that you have no idea how you're going to achieve it." So far so good. But then I had to actually make it happen.

So, in August 2018 on my 54th birthday I was running through my mind what the future would hold as I continued my biomechanical decline. It struck me that continuing to track downhill wasn't in any doubt, it was more a case of how fast and how far the decline would take me. It was then that I saw on Facebook the picture of me at the party. I would have been way too embarrassed to show it back then. Not the fact that I'm enjoying a glass of red wine, I'd been self-medicating with alcohol for as long as I can remember. Not even the cigarette. They'd helped me decompress and compose myself on many an occasion. No, I would have been embarrassed to tell you that "that guy" had taken on the challenge to compete in an IRONMAN® triathlon in 12 months. The gap between my current self-identity and where it would need to be in 12 months' time was so vast that nobody would believe it. Me included.

Stating, "I'm an IRONMAN® competitor" was delusional not motivational. That's not the guy that should be accepting that challenge. Adapt more to endure less. I may have convinced myself that I'd accepted the adventure but the disconnect between my goal and my identity was making it impossible to switch on the seeking system. Maybe you can relate to this. You want to take the next step on the career ladder, to take on that "aim high" objective, but it feels like you're talking about somebody else's goal. It just isn't you. So, you can understand that the provocation to find new strategies was extreme and immediate.

I had no strategies for that challenge. None. Everything was going to have to come out of the *potential drawer*! As it turned out it was the perfect opportunity to test the models within this book. I didn't realise at the time that *Unashamedly* was going to be equally as challenging as *Superhuman*.

Although this triathlon is clearly a before and after story, it has nothing to do with an external change. It's not a makeover story—frankly I don't look much different now; slightly smaller breasts perhaps. And I'm not trying to create any fake jeopardy; I told you at the start that I did it.

Slightly unconventionally, I ended up doing the whole thing on my own, two years later than planned. The first cancellation occurred six weeks before I was due to go to Copenhagen. I woke up in a ditch with an ambulance crew strapping me onto a stretcher after a wipe-out on a training ride. Cue three months off training. I regrouped and signed up for IRONMAN® Texas in April 2020. Well, we all know why that got cancelled. I rolled it over to April 2021. Same thing happened. By September 2021, I decided that waiting was no longer an option. I couldn't find an available event, so planned my own route: Caversham Lake for the 2.4-mile (3.9-km) swim, then hop on the bike, up and down the A4 between Reading and Maidenhead for 112 miles (180 km), then run four loops of 6.55 miles (10.54 km) to complete the marathon. Done.

I felt better at the end of the day than I did at the beginning. No injuries. No surgeries. It all sounds rather self-congratulatory. I don't mean it to. I thought long and hard about whether or not to include it in the book. However, the adventure that it took me on, particularly after the bike accident, resulted in me discovering some incredible performance hacks. I had to include it.

This private adventure provoked me to tap into an in-built system, one that we all share, and it taught me what our mind and body are capable of. In hindsight, the wipe-out on the bike was the best thing that ever happened to me.

What Doesn't Kill Us by Scott Carney was the book that I read when I was laid up nursing my injuries. It was a statement on the front cover that caught my attention. It says, "How freezing water, extreme altitude, and environmental conditioning, will renew our lost evolutionary strength." This, in particular, got my attention, "our lost evolutionary strength." I was in need of this *lost evolutionary strength* he talked about.

Carney is based in Denver, Colorado. He's an investigative journalist. He challenges charlatans and debunks them if they don't deliver on their promises. The Dutch extreme adventurer Wim Hof features heavily. After spending a month together in

Arctic conditions in Czechoslovakia, he determined that the promises made by Wim – that anyone could develop the ability to withstand the harshest possible external conditions—was indeed achievable.

Of course, the question that comes to mind is, why would you want to? Even if we could, which seems unlikely, why would we want to develop this freakish ability to swim in ice-cold water or hike for hours in blizzards wearing only boots and a pair of shorts? Well, hold that thought, we'll be coming back to that!

For now, think back to a time when you accepted a challenge. Either a challenge that was given to you or one that you set yourself. Something that would fit into the six- to 12-month time frame. Something you can look back on and think, yeah, that was a real stretch. It pushed me. Or you can think of something right now that you're going for. A goal that you're currently working on. Maybe you also have an aspiration and you're not sure whether you've even got what it takes to achieve it. Nonetheless, it's something that, if achieved, would make the next 12 months a tremendous investment in your life. Whether you're reflecting on a past achievement or considering a current goal I'd invite you to keep it front of mind whilst we explore the rest of the ADAPT process.

Okay, so if it's challenging you then good. If it's something you're passionate about achieving, better. Bringing challenge and passion together creates purpose and focuses the attention. Two qualities that will be essential as we press forward.

So, step 1, we **Accept the Adventure**. Step 2, we **Direct the Seeking System** and focus on our direction of travel, something that we want to achieve. That brings us to step 3, **Activate**. Activate what? Well, how about our lost evolutionary strength for starters.

Chapter 6

ACTIVATE THE NEW AND IMPROVED

For me, this was the most exciting part of Professor Peterson's definition of tapping potential: "There's more to you because you've tried something new. That's one thing. But the second thing is, there's good biological evidence for this now that if you put yourself in a new situation, then new genes code for new proteins and build new neural structures and new nervous system structures." If you put yourself in a new situation, then the stress, the situational stress, that's produced by that particular situation, unlocks those genes and then builds new parts of you.

In the context of ADAPT, *activate* means developing any new skills, disciplines, behaviours, or practices brought about by the demands of your adventure.

Consider this equation:

$$\text{Knowledge} + \text{Skills} + \text{Process} \times \text{Mindset} = \text{Performance}$$

When we are driving change and striving to adapt to new conditions or environments, there is likely to be a demand on us to develop some new capabilities. This simple formula provides a useful checklist to review our current position compared to our desired outcome. In other words, when you visualise your direction of travel what will you need to know more about that you don't right now? Are there any specific skills that you will need to develop? What are the supporting processes that will be in place in your desired future that aren't currently?

These are practical questions and the answers may be obvious to you. That said, the answers may be harder to pinpoint and relate more to psychological capabilities or mindsets. We'll be taking a deep dive into all things *mindset* in Part III of the book, but for now let's just define *mindset* as a word we use to describe the way in which we lean into any situation. You'll notice on the formula that mindset is positioned as having a multiplying effect. That's not to say that mindset is enough on its own. It isn't. There are many examples of people being super motivated, whilst lacking the necessary skills for the job.

When I left school at 16, I did a four-year mechanical engineering apprenticeship. I couldn't have been more motivated and I couldn't have been more clueless. I wasn't just an idiot, I was a highly motivated idiot! Dangerous around heavy machinery. Or consider TV shows like *X Factor*, particularly the early shows. The losing contestants dazed and confused after failing their audition protesting to the judges, "I'll be back" or "I'm going to be a star!" They then reveal their slightly flawed strategy for success: "because I WANT it." They want it! You can't fault their confidence. Frankly, their persistence is to be applauded. But wanting it just isn't good enough. We all want it. The spanner in the works in this instance is they simply can't sing! An important component given the competition they're in.

Perhaps a more difficult statement to grasp is that having the knowledge and skill alone isn't good enough either. Being good isn't good enough. I refer back to any situation where you've visited The Choke zone in the Edge Model in Figure 3.1. Visiting the bottom left hand quadrant can still happen to the very best. Professional footballers should never miss a penalty. Sure the goalkeeper could save it, but they should never miss the whole goal area! Professional golfers should never miss a 12-inch putt. Ever. But they do. Contestants on *Shark Tank* or *Dragon's Den,* who have prepared for months to deliver a five-minute pitch about something they invented, should never forget their own name, but they do, sometimes literally.

The point being that, in spite of the critical importance of developing the required knowledge, skills, and processes, the thing that determines whether we have access to our ability in the heat of the moment is our mindset. Of course, each has a pivotal role to play and $K + S + P \times M$ should all feature in our personal and professional development plans.

It's worth a mention here that whichever of the preceding requires development, I don't underestimate the amount of effort required to take on new and improved ways of operating. Sometimes even the most obvious changes in behaviour appear problematic when it comes to actually changing our behaviours.

Even if we know what needs to change, making it happen is far from easy. Often there is a gap between our common sense and our common practice. For example, most of us know the benefits of the following activities:

- Exercising 30–40minutes a day
- Drinking 2 litres (2.1 quarts) of water a day
- Sleeping seven hours or so a night
- Eating our 5 A Day portions of fruits and vegetables
- Chopping out smoking and limiting alcohol consumption to 14 units a week.
- Flossing

However, knowing what to do doesn't always equal doing what we know. In order to activate the new and improved, we must be prepared to swim against the current.

Swimming against the current

As the phrase infers, it's difficult. It's difficult because it's different, it's doing new things. It's not the way we *currently* do things. Adopting new behaviours requires a strategy that enables us to rewire old patterns and create new and improved alternatives.

Frankly, whenever we push ourselves through the learning curve we tend to experience four distinct phases. Typically it starts with unconscious incompetence. We don't know what we don't know. When we're teenagers watching parents or friends driving, we have no idea how difficult our first driving lesson is going to be. Looks pretty easy from where we're sitting. It soon becomes apparent, particularly with a stick-shift, when the instructor says, put your foot on that pedal, the clutch, then push that lever into first gear, next slowly release the clutch, and then put your foot on that pedal, the accelerator. Lift that lever, the indicator, whilst looking in the mirror to check your blind spot. "Do all of them?" you ask. "All at the same time," the instructor replies.

As you lurch off, kangarooing down the road, you transition to the second phase of learning. Conscious incompetence. You now know you don't know. It's a painful phase which challenges your beliefs about whether you can and will ever acquire this new skill. With a little practice however, and a little patience, you quickly move to phase three. Conscious competence. You now know you know how to do this. The fruits of your labour are paying off. But it takes focus and concentrated effort. "Foot on the clutch, into first, off the clutch, mirror, signal, manoeuvre, back on the clutch, into second...." The instructor then goes to say something and you snap, "Shhhhhh, don't speak!" A hundred percent of your cognitive ability is being used up; there's no room for any more.

Psychologists call it *7+ or −2*, meaning our conscious mind can only manage seven areas of focus at any one time before steam comes out of our ears. This can be increased to nine if we're in a particularly resourceful state or reduced to five if you're already a little stressed going in. This phase is where the work really begins. This is where you find out how much you want it. You do, so you persevere, and there comes a point in time where everything clicks into place. We rarely know when it happened; we just know we don't have to think about it any more. Unconscious competence. The cognitive function of driving is now being directed by your unconscious mind enabling you to apply your 7+ or −2 to other things like listening to the radio, thinking about the meeting you're headed to, and eating your sandwich.

Back to the driving lesson, when you arrive you have no recollection of anything else that happened en-route. When it comes to replacing the old behaviours with the new and improved, it's particularly important to understand the effort required to turn a conscious choice to do something into an unconscious, habitual way of doing things. Advertisers understand this. They know that in order to influence our choices and cause us to change our brand selection, they need to recondition our thinking. Logic will help, but it's not enough. Creating a positive association at an unconscious level is the thing that gets their product in our shopping trolly.

You might doubt that you are actually being conditioned at an unconscious level. Other people, sure, but not you. The challenge lies in the word *unconscious*. We don't know it's happening. Try this. Depending on where you are in the world will determine your response to the following. What comes next?

Beanz meanz...

A Mars a day helps you... ... ...

How about if I said, *You're worth it,* which brand would I be referring to?

So here's how it works. *You're out shopping for groceries and you head for the canned goods aisle. You want baked beans. There are five different brands. As you scan the options, the little voice in your head says, "I think you'll find Beanz meanz Heinz." Whose choice was that? Who decided it would be good for Heinz to be the first word to come into your head after we think of beans? There are five different brands. As we scan the options, the little voice in our head says, "I think you'll find Beanz meanz Heinz." Whose choice was that? Who decided it would be good for Heinz to be the first word to come into our head after we think of beans?*

Yes, that would have been Heinz's choice. The Mars campaign is even more impressive. *A Mars a day helps you work, rest, and play.* Oh, really? Does it? Nutritionally? I don't think so. I think you'll find that what ticks all those boxes would be a banana. It hasn't even got to be true but unconsciously we still connect the brand with the influential strapline.

First and foremost marketers understand it's not just conscious "logical reasoning" that drives our decisions, it's more about the emotional, unconscious associations we make. So, in the 30-second duration of the advert, whether or not we were paying attention, their strategy is to use any necessary means to boost our "mood" through music, humour, jingles, or catchphrases. A little help from celebrities always adds a little credibility too. They're looking for whatever it takes to create an immediate "feel good factor," which unconsciously gets connected to their brand. The companies have one sole purpose in mind: When the time comes to choose, choose them.

Even though the tactics of yesteryear were nowhere near as sophisticated as the psychology-savvy marketers of today, 20 years on, I still only buy Heinz beans, a Mars bar is my first choice of sporty chocolate snack, and my daughters still insist on L'Oréal.

So, in the context of pushing yourself to acquire new knowledge, skills, processes and mindsets, it might be helpful to have some strategies that will enable you to remain calm, focused and driven, whilst working through the challenge of behavioural change. Let's look at how to "hack" our own conditioned response.

The key word in the question is *conditioned.* I spent some time with someone in the Special Forces and when we were talking about performing under pressure he said something that stuck with me: "When you're under pressure you don't rise to the occasion, you fall to the level of your conditioning." That's an interesting way of looking at things. I always thought when you were under pressure, you would raise your game by gearing up and getting psyched-up but he said, no. When the heat is on, you're going to fall to the level of your conditioning, and of course, we are conditioned to respond. We have our own habitual patterns, ways of thinking and ways of behaving. So, in terms of how you rewire or recondition that response we need some specific tools to help us both in the moment and when we're preparing ourselves for those upcoming moments that matter. The person who comes to mind who has broken this down into user-friendly tools and techniques is American Neuroscientist and Professor of Neurobiology at the Stanford University of Medicine, Andrew Huberman. I like his take on neuroscience because it's very practical and pragmatic.

Professor Huberman talks about real-time tools, which are based on neurons and neural circuits. In other words, things we've all got built into us. There's no learning involved. Once you know how to activate them, you just do it. And you just see what happens. These are tools we can gain access to help us to decompress, to reset, and recondition the way we feel. So instead of trying to change what's happening in the outside world we change how we're responding to it.

Chapter 7

PERSIST
PERSIST
PERSIST

What are the gyms like in January? Can't get a machine at 7 a.m. in January. What are the gyms like around late February, early March? Not so busy! Every year people around the world make New Year's resolutions to reach their goals, improve their health, and better their lives. Many people are successful at keeping their resolutions, while many others fail.

Of those who make a New Year's resolution, after one week 75 percent are still successful in keeping it. After two weeks, the number drops to 71 percent. After one month, the number drops again to 64 percent. And after six months, 46 percent of people who make a resolution are still successful in keeping it. In comparison, of those people who have similar goals but do not set a resolution, only 4 percent are still successful after six months.[1]

According to a 2016 study, of the 41 percent of those who make New Year's resolutions, by the end of the year only 9 percent feel they are successful in keeping them. It would seem that just setting the goal with positive intentions isn't enough to get the job done. Persistence is required. Let me offer a neuroscience take on persistence and provide a fail-safe performance hack to guarantee success when the New Year comes around again.

Think back to the images of the ice bath and the very different experiences being felt by our two bathers. The observation we're making is that, in the moment at least, the gentleman on the left is having to put in a significant amount more effort than the young woman who has somehow managed to adapt to the external environment. To follow the ADAPT model, she's accepted, redirected her focus, and in doing so, activated some in-built resources. As a result, it would appear that her need for persistence is somewhat less than his. So, let's hop out of the ice and return to the demands of our own challenge.

More than likely during the adaptation process our ability to persist will likely be the difference that makes the difference.

---

[1] "New Year's Resolution Statistics," (2021 Updated, 2022), *Discover Happy Habits*, 3 February. Available at: https://discoverhappyhabits .com/new-years-resolution-statistics/.

Finishing the book you've started? Completing an online learning course? Developing a deeper understanding of the various personality types that make up your team, their individual motivators and needs? Or getting a grip of all things virtual as we move into a new paradigm for engaging and interacting with each other? Or is it more to do with developing specific skills? People skills perhaps? Communicating with impact and precision. Or is it more to do with honing critical thinking skills and problem solving skills? Or it could be a process issue that needs to be addressed; maybe project management, performance management, or you're in the middle of implementing a new customer relationship management system. Thinking back to the Performance Model, wherever the demand is—Knowledge, Skills, or Process—perhaps the determining factor that will make the biggest difference will be your ability to influence yourself and others to stay in an optimum Mindset, aka to remain in the top left hand quadrant on the Edge model. Specifically, I'm talking about your ability to manage, handle, and utilise stress.

In March 2020 a friend from the London Business School, John Dore, posted on LinkedIn, "I've just been disrupted. Overnight I've become Blockbuster, Kodak, and the Diesel engine." He wasn't the only one. All over the world, across every business sector, the VUCA world was sending stress levels through the roof. Some suffered, struggled, and began what was to become their greatest test of endurance, but our focus here is the others who were able to quickly adapt. In order to progress through the change curve, and maintain the necessary energy to keep moving forward, they would have had a dependable strategy for dealing with the brain's automatic stress response that was in full alert mode. If that was you, you'll recognise yourself in this next section.

If, like me, the alarm bells caused an overwhelming sense of distraction, confusion, and distress, then keep reading because we're now going to explore a strategy that will ensure clarity, focus, and drive should it ever happen again.

It's probably safe to say that humans are the curators of the Earth. We're the species in charge. We're not the strongest; we can't jump as high or run as fast as many the other species, but the main reason we're afforded this lofty position is because of certain capabilities of our brains; two in particular – the ability to plan and to implement plans. Because our brain and nervous system are terrifically adaptive machines, we are able to modify our behaviours, our thoughts, our emotions, and ultimately, our actions so that we continually build out technologies that allow us to adapt faster and faster and faster. We don't just focus on what's in our immediate environment. We have elements of our wiring that are designed to do that, but more importantly, and specifically relevant when focusing on persistence, is something known as the dopamine system. It's a powerful driver and force for us.

Dopamine is a chemical that's released in the brain. It's best known as the reward chemical. It's released anytime we achieve anything important to us – passing your driving test or the moment you see the straight A's on your exam results; achieving a pay rise or the promotion you've worked hard for; or finally being allowed out after lockdown. It's associated with big win type of events. But what's less appreciated is that dopamine has a much more powerful role when pursuing goals, particularly when the desire is to adapt more in order to endure less.

Mother Nature installed this feel-good chemical for anytime we're focused on something outside our immediate reach. It drives goal direction not just goal attainment. It's like a thruster and it keeps us motivated when we're working towards a degree or a promotion, or building a business. It's an amazing mechanism because it not only keeps us focused on the external goal, but it also ensures we feel good while we're en-route to that goal. It seems humans need a reward system to help them enjoy the journey as well as the destination. That's the dopamine system.

So far so good; however, you'll also be familiar with another equally powerful brain chemical: adrenaline. It's technically called noradrenaline but let's use the more familiar name. Adrenaline is associated with the effort process, whether that's related to the effort of running a marathon or running a business. Here's the important bit; it turns out there's a circuit in the brain that is counting off and measuring how much adrenaline is present. And when you exert for long enough and there's no dopamine, it triggers a quitting reflex. It literally triggers the sensation of "I've had enough. I can't keep going. I'm done." No doubt we've all experienced that before. Of course, in those moments where we just have to stop, whether that's an extended bout of exercise or the sixth Zoom meeting in a row, we could simply put it down to physical fatigue.

However, consider the scenes at the end of a football match. 0–0 at full time. 0–0 after extra time. The penalty shoot-out determines the victors and losers. Seconds later the runners-up have collapsed all over the pitch, seeking medical attention for cramping whilst the winners are doing a lap of honour, on each other's shoulders! We can safely assume that players from both sides gave everything they had in pursuit of victory, yet it would appear that one team is completely burnt out whilst the other has been given rocket fuel. Or to put it another way, one team has overdosed on adrenaline whilst the other just received a massive dose of dopamine. In our language we call it a *second wind*.

Have you ever had one of those nights where, no matter what you try, you just can't get off to sleep, and are tossing and turning. Finally you drop off only to hear your alarm go off. It's 4 a.m. and time to get up. In a haze, you suddenly remember your all-expenses-paid, first-class flight to Mauritius leaves at 7 a.m. and your limo is picking you up in an hour. How are your energy levels? I'm guessing pretty good! So, how can we control this game-changing energy-boosting system to help us to keep going when driving to achieve our goal of adapting to ever-evolving and sometimes stressful external environments? An example that's often used to help us to both understand, and more importantly take control of the two internal systems that can cause us to either crash and burn or push on with energy and vigour, is the candidate selection process used by our special forces.

Perhaps the first thing to recognise is that the would-be commandos are expected to provide their own motivation; their own dopamine. I'm reliably informed there's no café latte and doughnuts at the start of manoeuvres. People who get through find those rewards internally. So why quit? Whether running or embarking on long bouts of work, when we exert, effort adrenaline is released in our brain. At some point if there is too much, it trips a switch and shuts down our ability to think straight and function. The thing that resets it to a manageable level and gives us more gas is dopamine.

Dopamine has the ability to take that level of adrenaline, smack it down, and give us the time and energy to continue. It's as if we are giving ourselves permission to keep going. Fortunately, we have the capacity as humans to self-dose dopamine. The reward system is entirely internal and it's our ability to focus on wins throughout the day that create the necessary momentum. I'm not talking about positive self-talk. Positive self-talk is often linked to the end goal. Thinking about crossing the finish line at the end of an IRONMAN® race, or any long day for that matter, is fine when the end is in sight, when it's in striking distance but of no value at 6 a.m. when starting the lake swim. If I'm losing and I say I'm winning, I know I'm lying. No dopamine is released.

This performance hack is called self-rewarding. The idea is to reward the effort process. Rewarding yourself at every milestone, it registers as a partial win. It's like a "feel good" dopamine drip feed. This performance hack is called self-rewarding. The idea is to reward the effort process. Rewarding yourself at every milestone, it registers as a partial win. It's like a "feel good" dopamine drip feed. As soon as we learn that we set the amount of internal reward, we realise we have an infinite amount of energy to pursue our goals.

We experience it as the ability to push through the pain. If you learn to do it when running or pushing through to the end of a deep work session or enduring a cold shower, you can transfer the ability to other areas of life because it's the same circuits that are involved. Persistence relates to the journey, not the destination.

Let's look at some techniques that can help us to self-reward whilst we're en-route to achieving our goals.

Performance hack: Thin slicing recognition

To generate more energy and more focus, let's look at the self-reward aspects of the process.

Remind yourself that you are on track and look for tiny digestible chunks in order to continue moving forward. Think of the special forces selection process; everyone shows up fit and full of grit. They all believe they will make it through, but only a small subset do. Determination is necessary but not sufficient. They aren't necessarily failed by the instructors, they self-select. They quit. They quit because they can't manage their brain chems. Those that make it through are able to control something in their internal environment whilst not being in control of their external environment. They do this in the most demanding circumstances – sleep deprived, immersed in cold water, under interrogation when tired and depleted of energy. It's in those moments that the ones who are able to reward themselves get that bit of extra gas to keep forward momentum. The result? They don't quit.

It's not resilience. It's attaching a sense of meaning to what they are doing. It's micro-slicing the day and narrowing the focus, for example, getting to the next lamppost on a challenging run. They don't need to understand the adrenaline/dopamine battle that's going on in their brain. They just need to know the power of the self-reward process. The key message here is central to the theme of *Unashamedly Superhuman* – that anyone can tap into these circuits. Not just ultra-distance athletes. Not just special forces operatives. Anyone can. The ultimate determinant isn't physical; it's chemical.

So, let's assume you're on the dopamine train. You've got goals that you're building towards. You're not only looking forward to the dopamine you'll get when you cross the finish line, but you've also been thin slicing recognition and getting a little bit of dopamine for the journey. Your high-performance chemicals are all topped up. So, how about some well-being chemicals too? Mother Nature installed another reward mechanism. This one releases the feel-good chemicals serotonin and oxytocin which generate a sense of peace and calm. They're literally heart-warming because they trigger neural circuits that link the gut and brain and create a sense of warmth in the torso. A feeling of well-being. These are designed to be released when we hold a loved one or when we're around close friends. Sometimes, even when we look at objects that hold meaning for us like a sentimental piece of jewelry or a lucky charm. They're literally heart-warming because they trigger neural circuits that link the gut and brain, and they create a sense of warmth in the torso. A feeling of well-being. It's how I feel about my dog. I look at her and I just feel good. I have no reason to be anywhere else at that moment to get a feel-good feeling. Serotonin and oxytocin generate a sense of peace and calm.

It is vitally important for anyone who is ambitious and hard-working to understand that both reward mechanisms: dopamine/adrenaline, which help drive us forward, and serotoin/oxytocin, which help us to appreciate where we are right now. Helping us to both work towards things and then gain a deep appreciation and satisfaction for what you have.

Performance hack: Gratitude

Gratitude also keeps the adrenaline at bay by buffering the quit reflex. When the going got really tough, it was this hack that got me through my 12-and-half-hour endurance event. As important as purpose, focus, and determination were, which we'll come to in Part III – Tapping into Mindset, and physiological conditioning, which we'll explore in Part IV – Tapping into Physiology, these were not the tools that got me through. Before 2 September

2021, I wouldn't have considered including gratitude practices it in this book. I'd never read about it, never talked about it, and hadn't planned it into my strategy. Without any doubt, I hadn't anticipated the power that could be had from adopting an attitude of gratitude. I'd misunderstood it. For years I would roll my eyes at the cheesy Instagram posts that pop up almost daily.

"No duty is more urgent than giving thanks." —James Allen

"Gratitude is not only the greatest of virtues but the parent of all others." —Cicero

They smacked of complacency and navel gazing. The lightbulb moments came deep into the six-hour bike ride when I found myself focusing on how fortunate I was to be in a position where I could be testing myself to this extent, compared to the physical position I'd found myself in 12 months earlier when lying in a ditch. I lost count of the number of times I said out loud, "Thank you." In the moment, I had no real idea who or what I was thanking, but I do know the feeling it generated carried me through the 26-mile (42-km) run.

Gratitude is fundamentally different from complacency because of the neurochemical signature of gratitude. For example, there are neuroimaging studies that support the idea that a short period of stillness each day, anywhere from five to zero minutes combined with some gratitude practice, creates a neurochemical signature in us that involves dopamine release as well as serotonin and oxytocin. That combination is very powerful because all at once you feel good and you feel capable. This sensation gives you a this feeling of possibility, and yet you're happy with yourself. I confused gratitude with something that would make me want less. When you dig a little deeper and see people who are really driven, but have kept that up over time, what you'll often find is they practice gratitude.

Chapter 8

TUNE IN/ TUNE UP

When we adapt we are becoming adjusted to new conditions. We accept the adventure to direct our seeking system
in order to shift our focus in a predetermined direction, our
direction of travel. We activate new and improved approaches,
and we are prepared to persist in moving forward. Finally, we
can commit to refining our approach on an ongoing basis. We'll
call that tune in and tune up.

Tune in/Tune up

I received a most unusual invitation to speak to a select group of
people. All I knew was they were part of the armed forces—
special forces as it turned out. It was unusual because I had no
briefing call. Just an invitation: *Turn up at the following address.
Your session runs from 1 p.m. to 2.30 p.m.* I was intrigued.

On arrival I was met by the officer in charge. He said, "Are
you ready?" I explained that it was unusual to not have a briefing
call but that I was indeed ready to go. "What do you want to
know?" he asked. I said that normally I would ask what it was that
the group I'm going to be working with did on a day-to-day basis,
but that on this occasion that would seem like a stupid question.
He agreed. It caught me slightly off guard and without really
thinking I said, "So what makes you special? What's the difference between special and ordinary forces?" It wasn't a serious
question, more tongue in cheek. But his reply was serious.

*No matter how intense the circumstances, no matter how demanding
or chaotic, we notice everything that's going on around us...and when I
say everything, I mean everything! As a result, we make finer distinc-
tions and better decisions.* Good answer.

We entered the conference room. There were five round
tables. Three at the front of the room that, it soon became clear,
were populated by the special forces, and two tables set back a
little that it turned out were made up of some of the support
functions at the camp. The leader opened up the session and
mentioned to the group the very brief "briefing" that had taken
place outside. "This is Jim, our guest speaker. He just asked me
a question and I'd like to test the answer I gave him."

He then asked me to select one of the team from one of the front three tables. I gestured across the room towards one of the servicemen. Let's call him Mike. He was asked to come to the front of the room and was instructed to stand with his face up against the wall with his back to the room. Eyes closed.

I was then invited to ask Mike anything about the room. Anything that he may have noticed. What followed was astonishing! The first thing I noticed were the people in the room so I asked, "How many people are there here?"

Without taking a breath, he said, "42, including you. Too easy"

I wasn't going to count them.... He seemed confident.

I rationalised that he must have seen the delegate list beforehand and made a note of the number in attendance. Second question, "How many chairs are there?" I'd noticed that there were several spare chairs dotted around the room.

"49," he replied, instantly. Correct again.

Question three, "How many pictures are there on the walls?"

When he answered nine I was impressed, even though I'd only counted eight. Pretty close. But then he followed up with, "If you include the fire instructions which are in a frame by the door." OK, I thought, he knows the room. Maybe they've played this game before. Maybe it was the party trick for the visitor.

"Try again," said his boss, who was clearly enjoying how things were going. Starting to understand the game I figured the one thing he wouldn't know anything about was me. Question five, "What colour shirt am I wearing?" As I was wearing a jumper over my shirt with just the V-neck and collar showing, I thought I may have taken it too far.

Nope. Mike replied "Blue and white pinstripe, three millimetre (referring to the width of the stripes)." I didn't even know!

My next question turned out to be the finale. I'd recently had my eyes tested and I suddenly became aware of the people in the room wearing glasses. Surely not. How many people are wearing glasses, I asked. I'd counted seven. "Eight," he said, "If you include John who took his off 10 minutes ago." A guy at the back of the room shouted, "Where did I put them?" Left-hand shirt pocket was the reply. John duly peeled them out of his left-hand shirt pocket. I started to applaud, as did the two tables at the back of the room.

Not the front three tables. They just sat there like it was the most natural thing in the world. Mike took a seat. I was invited to speak, but before I started I said how impressive his performance was. "Not really," he said. "You could have picked any one of us, it would have been the same." I then asked the obvious question. How? How do you do it? His answer was also obvious whilst artfully vague, "We're trained to." I wasn't expecting any specifics.

The point being they made a proactive decision to put a spotlight on a critical success factor and hone that processing ability to ensure they are acutely aware of all relevant information that connects to their performance.

Of course, it's a success habit that applies to more than just elite members of the military. The more we can tune into the things that matter most, the key skills and behaviours that determine the quality of our performance, and participate in practices that develop that core capability, the more control we have over our response to the challenges that we'll encounter in our pursuit to adapt. We need to train our brain for success.

Think about what happened in the early stages of the pandemic. First off we were glued to the TV. Viewing figures at the BBC, SKY, CNN, and Fox went through the roof. If you were feeling overwhelmed and exhausted it's no surprise because you were doing more cerebral processing than usual. Way more thinking. It used to be that you got up, brushed your teeth, checked your phone, grabbed coffee, and you went about your day. Suddenly we had to think about whether or not you could touch a door handle, how you were going to get groceries. There was a lot more planning and so we were allocating a lot more time and energy to our thinking brain, our prefrontal cortex.

We were having to think a lot harder and devote a lot more energy to things that we just didn't even have to think about before. The brain consumes an immense amount of energy, far more than running. So now we were running mental marathons every day. People vary tremendously in their capacity for these sorts of mental operations. Some people are just trained up in them, and some people aren't. Even so, it seemed everyone was a little more depleted than usual. What was really happening was we were in deep modes of uncertainty. Whenever that's the case, the brain wants to figure out three things:

- Duration, how long something's going to last.
- Path, how to get there.
- Outcome, what is going to happen?

What was unique at that time was that nobody knew the answer to each of those three key questions. So, as we navigate change and focus on adaptation, if the answer to duration, path or outcome is unclear, the nervous system will be working overtime and we experience that as stress. In such circumstances what we can all do is start to cultivate practices that bring us to the best possible emotional state, the top left-hand quadrant. We need to give ourselves a chance to filter the information in front of us, which is the ability to restore yourself in order to have more energy for when you need it. Mike and the team made a proactive decision to put a spotlight on a critical success factor and hone that processing ability to ensure they are acutely aware of all relevant information that connects to their performance. Let's take a minute to do the same and tune up our ability to tackle stress.

Stress busting

Chapter 7 focuses our attention on the quit reflex and the remarkable ability we have to buffer it by triggering a release of dopamine to suppress the stress response. So as we tune in on this critical ability, let me offer up a series of simple tune-up performance hacks to help us to quickly de-stress.

Essentially we experience two types of stress: acute and chronic. Acute is short term and intense, while chronic is less intense but long lasting. One of the reasons that stress can be such a drain on our energy is its pervasive nature. It can colour how we see everything else around us. All of a sudden minor things that wouldn't normally bother us can get to us too. You know when you're having "one of those days" when all it takes to tip you over the edge is someone using your favourite coffee cup. So, what can we do about it?

First, when it comes to peak performance, I'm going to simplify things and say there is only one state of mind that we ever really need to be in; a combination of feeling both calm and alert. But how? How do you stay both calm and alert in this sometimes crazy world?

There are two types of strategies or tools for dealing with stress. The first type are those that push the stress level down before it really kicks in. Here, we prevent the *quit reflex* from cutting in and draining our energy. We've looked at two self-rewarding hacks; thin-slicing recognition when we're on the *path* and adopting gratitude practices. The second type of strategies are those that reduce the stress response after it's already been activated. Here, we can prevent the build-up of the stress hormone cortisol and the disempowering feelings that can come with it. OK, here are three hacks you can tune up with.

Performance hack: Create more stress!

Yeah, that's what I thought when I heard that piece of wisdom... more stress? The key point is it has to be the right kind of stress, stay with me.

Apparently short, intentional (and that's the important bit, intentional) bursts of acute stress can be really effective for reducing chronic stress. For example, a short, intense workout...just 10 or 15 minutes. Jumping into cold water is also highly recommended. People who engage in cold-water swimming during the winter months swear by it. Even a 15-second cold shower triggers endorphins that boost the immune system. More on that later. It certainly interrupts your train of thought!

And that's partly the theory.... Short bursts of intense activity seem to help break the pattern of thinking that can facilitate worry and anxiety.

If that seems a bit extreme, this second hack is more logical. We did this when we talked about Acceptance. Accept the problem to accept the challenge to accept the adventure.

Performance hack: Mindful reframing

This is a great way to stress-bust.

An interesting study done at the University of Wisconsin found that individuals who experienced a high level of stress throughout their life, but viewed stress as a trigger for growth and development, had dramatically lower rates of illness than individuals who experienced less stress, but viewed it as a bad thing!

In other words, the "frame" we wrap around our experience can affect how negatively or positively the stress impacts us. What if the stress we're dealing with is seen as something that's causing us to grow stronger? Well, science would say that it actually will.

However, what if you don't have 15 minutes for a burst of intentional stress or the time to think through an empowering reframe, what if you're about to jump on a Zoom call and you can feel the stress building, what can you do that is fast and effective?

Well, then we have our final stress-buster....

Performance hack: The physiological sigh

As Stanford's Professor Huberman says, "This is one straight from Mother Nature." It's a technique that pretty much all animals do when they're falling asleep, when they are relaxing or destressing. If you have a pet, watch it when it's settling down for a nap. Just before it fully relaxes it breathes in, then breathes in a bit more, then it breathes out like a long sigh. We do it too, but typically just when we're dropping off to sleep, so we're not aware of it. When children are getting to the end of an anger tantrum, just before they start to calm down, they do it. This simple breathing hack triggers a rapid relaxation response.

We can do it to cancel the stress response after it's already been activated. It buys us a moment of control before we respond. The best time to test it is right after you feel a surge of stress. It's a simple breathing practice that triggers the calming reflex. This has to do with the exchange of oxygen and carbon dioxide in the lungs and bloodstream. If you want to calm down slowly, you could eat a big meal or you could take a long walk, but if you want to calm down quickly, you want to trigger the activation of a specific set of neurons in the brainstem that are actually responsible for sighing.

We don't realise it, but subconsciously throughout the day, and during sleep, we do something where we inhale twice, and then we do a long exhale. You take a big deep inhale through your nose, and then at the top, you're going to inhale again, and then you exhale through your mouth. It immediately balances the ratio of carbon dioxide and oxygen in the lungs and bloodstream properly, and it triggers activation of the sigh neurons, which have a direct and fast route to what we're calling the calming circuit. If repeated several times, you will naturally restore a level of calm.

So, just before an important Zoom presentation, or if somebody cuts in front of you in traffic, or whatever else it is that flips that switch take a long, deep breath in through your nose and when it feels like you can't breathe in any more, quickly sniff again. Then immediately breathe out through your mouth. A long steady exhale. The science says when you sniff the second time, these tiny sacs in your lungs snap open, increasing the oxygen going in, but also the carbon dioxide coming out, which activates the part of our nervous system that causes us to feel calm.

Try it out .... Just pop a couple in before it's show-time. Super simple, but super helpful. Bang for buck, it's tremendous value. Of course, it in and of itself doesn't address the thing that's stressing us, but it will provoke a shift in our state, giving us a better chance of engaging in a more resourceful response.

These hacks may not sound like game-changers. They may just give us an extra 5 percent, a marginal gain, but marginal gains add up over time. Training the brain a little and often creates patterns and habits that can become the difference that makes the difference.

Sirs Brailsford and Hoy's marginal gains

At an event in London I had the great pleasure of interviewing Sir David Brailsford, British Cycling Performance Director and Sir Chris Hoy, one of the most decorated sportspeople in the world. They each shared their own take on high performance, but the one thing they both referenced as a fundamental element for their success and that of the teams they either led or were part of was a commitment to the philosophy of marginal gains.

On the concept of marginal gains, Sir David explained; "The whole principle came from the idea that if you broke down everything you could think of that goes into riding a bike, and then improved it by 1 percent, you will get a significant increase when you put them all together." In other words, it is the aggregation of a number of small gains that result in a large gain in overall performance, which can be significant in terms of achievement and outcomes. Brailsford sums it up: "Put simply...how small improvements in a number of different aspects of what we do can have a huge impact on the performance of the team."

The marginal gains philosophy brings many benefits, from productivity to sustainable growth, resulting in unlimited personal development. Any team, sporting or otherwise, that embraces the power of marginal gains is more likely to rise to the top and stay there. Deciphering the theory of marginal gains has become essential for out-running, out-climbing, and out-earning competitors, resulting in interest from sports psychologists and business consultants alike. When Sir David Brailsford was appointed Performance Director of British cycling, he faced an uphill battle. The team had been struggling to perform; limited by its "big picture" view of winning, the team had failed to reach the Olympic podium for several decades. By addressing each athlete's individual needs, he developed a team that went on to dominate Olympic competition. The marginal gains philosophy approaches failure and weaknesses as opportunities for growth, not points of criticism, improving the emotional well-being of athletes and employees alike. The team grows in a way that best suits its needs.

Win Learn Change

In 1990, a new tennis tournament was formed called the Grand Slam Cup. It was played at the end of the season at the Olympiahalle in Munich, Germany. The event was organised by the International Tennis Federation, which invited the best-performing players in the year's Grand Slam events (namely, the Australian Open, French Open, Wimbledon, and US Open) to compete. Throughout its existence, it was famous for paying out the highest prize money of any tournament in tennis: $2 million (£1,534,884) with another $1 million (£767,442) bonus if the winner had also won a Grand Slam event that year. Everyone wanted to win it. In particular, the home player Boris Becker.

Becker hit the scene in 1985 at Wimbledon when, as a 17-year-old unseeded player, he defeated South African Kevin Curren to take the title. It wasn't until 1994 that Becker made it to the final of the Grand Slam championship. He was up against Pete Sampras, the No. 1 ranked player in the world at the time. Becker won the first set, but Sampras upped his game and took the $2-million prize-winning championship three sets to one. It was during the postmatch interview that Becker said something that would change my life as a salesman.

It was 10 years later that a colleague and I were in the business lounge at Heathrow airport waiting for a flight to Frankfurt when Boris walked in and sat at the table behind us. I explained to my colleague that after his defeat to Sampras the interviewer asked him how he felt having got so close to fulfilling his ambition to be Grand Slam champion? Naturally, everybody watching expected him to be deflated and disappointed at being so close to winning the trophy, not to mention the $2 million. But no, none of it. Of course he wasn't happy he'd lost, but the surprising thing was his answer never referred to the fact that that was indeed the case.

Instead of dwelling on the result of the match, he instead tuned into the performance; the path not the outcome. He said that he was surprised by a particular element of Sampras' game. The American's ability to slice the ball to keep it low and Becker's inability to respond had been a deciding factor. "It won't next time," he said. Then came the killer line: "I may not have beaten him today but I believe I have learned how to, and that's worth more than $2 million to me."

Even in a win or lose sport, he wasn't playing a win-or-lose game. He was playing a win-or-learn game. It's a subtle but profound difference. One of Boris's strengths was that he rarely, if ever, dropped into the bottom left-hand quadrant. He didn't choke. He was known as *Boom Boom Becker*. He went for everything. Always 100 percent and 100 miles an hour. Choking is essentially brought on by fear. Fear of failure. Fear of making a mistake, or doing or saying something we might regret. We tighten up and invariably screw up. Becker took fear out of the equation.

Let me ask you, do you like to lose? Obviously not. Do you like to win? Of course. Do you like to learn? Sure no problem.

Taking this simple mind game back to my role of a rookie salesman radically changed the way I felt as I approached a new prospect or any new challenge. As I say, it changed my life. I felt the need to tell him, so I did. I asked him how he developed such a winning mindset. He talked about some of the coaches he'd had that had helped him, one in particular, Romanian Ion Ţiriac. A gritty player in his day, he helped him to realise that applying a win or learn-how-to-win approach to the game was not only an effective way to eradicate a fearful state, but also a process for continuous improvement.

Now, of course, many of the world's greatest sportspeople are trained to use the *Win Learn Change* model to process failure literally in the moment. That is where they reflect on a situation where they didn't achieve the result they wanted, they missed the penalty or dropped the ball but instead of interpreting the outcome as a loss, a mistake or a failure, they rapidly shift into "learning" mode. They extract the critical information that affected their performance, process it, and then move on. The point being, it's difficult to be stressed when learning is the worst-case scenario!

Back in our world, although we're totally aware of the fact that we didn't get the win we wanted, we didn't hit our target or achieve the desired result, if the word *lose* is removed from the equation and replaced by *learn*, our brain doesn't get the signal to release cortisol, the stress hormone. If we see our losses through that filter, there is nothing to fear as we approach our next challenge. As a result, we're much more likely to have access to our cognitive and physical capability, and equally more likely to bounce back and turn our losses into learns and subsequently more wins.

Performance hack: Keep a Win Learn Change journal

When coaching my clients we use this fundamental hack in order to tune in and raise awareness and then tune up by working on the learning experiences and changing the approach moving forward. It can help to answer the following questions:

1. What were my wins? (Write down anything that went according to plan. Everything you did well. Big and small.)
2. What were my learns? (Reflect on the things that didn't go so well. If you could go back, what might you do differently next time? Pinpoint some of the lessons learned.)
3. What will I change? (Given the information gathered, what one change will you make?)

Taking a few minutes, a few times a week, to answer these three simple questions will provide essential insights when focusing on performance improvement. This is the case whether working on gaining more knowledge, developing skills, implementing processes, or changing our mindset.

It's important to write down your answers. The process of putting pen to paper enables a higher level of thinking and, therefore, more focused action. When your brain isn't busy remembering everything, your brain can then process anything. It's when you're not overwhelmed that you become free to intellectually analyse and ask important questions. It's not just general recall that improves when you write things down. Writing it down will also improve your recall of the really important information. It doesn't just help you remember, it makes your mind more efficient by helping you focus on the truly important stuff. By writing down your answers, you will also see some interesting patterns emerge.

Focusing, even briefly, on the wins releases dopamine. Not just the successful results that you may have achieved (Outcome), but also the wins along the way (Path). Over time, the brain builds stronger and stronger associations to the behaviours, mindsets, and results that you recognise, making them more desirable and easier to repeat. What if the same thing keeps showing up when you reflect on the question "What are my learns?" Clearly we're not doing what is necessary to implement change.

If you apply this Win Learn Change hack unashamedly, over the course of the next 30 days whilst trying out some of the other hacks in this book, one thing I can promise you is this: progress!

Change is neither good nor bad, it simply is. It can be greeted with terror or joy, a tantrum that says 'I want it the way it was' or a dance that says "look, something new." Don Draper (*Mad Men*)

My final word on the VUCA world...

Is it possible to feel excited by the unprecedented times that we're in? Generally people are afraid to offer this as a moment of opportunity. What if we value the beauty of uncertainty? When you look at people who are unskilled at something, uncertainty is very high. As they become skilled, their certainty becomes higher. And when people achieve levels of mastery, obviously both certainty and skill are very high. They know that they've mastered something. You can invite uncertainty back as an opportunity to perform at levels that you wouldn't otherwise. Without uncertainty, we're just going to get more of the same. People who invite uncertainty back into their life or into their business, or whatever it is, are really saying, "I want that higher tier of existence."

When uncertainty shows up, it's perceived as interesting. It's an opportunity to really dance with something new, and create something new internally or externally. It's the opportunity to learn how to lead a company or work closely with a team to overcome something that they've never overcome before. Instead of focusing on trying to get back to the way things were, embrace uncertainty and discard the discomfort that comes from not being able to control things. It's the uncertainty that allows us to derive some dopamine from figuring things out.

Is it too optimistic to believe that when we come out of a period of Volatility, Uncertainty, Complexity, and Ambiguity, for example post-pandemic, there could be a beautiful new age of optimism for society? The new normal isn't going to look like it was before. We have to embrace that. And when I say we have to embrace that, I don't mean it just from a purely psychological standpoint, for all the neurochemical reasons. We have to look at it as a new way of interacting with the old things, like a deeper appreciation of the things that we had before and took for granted.

Whether or not we emerge from the experience stronger is going to depend on whether we can take on that mindset. We have to stay focused on not just the resilience piece to get through it, but on what we're gaining.

OPPORTUNITY IS NOWHERE
OPPORTUNITY IS *NOWHERE*
OPPORTUNITY IS *NOW HERE*

Part III

SMARTER – TAPPING INTO MINDSET

Mindset, and more specifically cultivating the right mindset, is a term that's been thrown around a great deal in relation to high performance. When sports stars fail to perform, their mindset is often under the spotlight. When people react negatively to a situation, it's their mindset that's questioned. What about you? Do you ever question your own mindset?

Do you even beat yourself up for having the "wrong" mindset? This part of the book explores our mindsets in detail (spoiler: we have more than one!) and look at how tapping into the right one at the right time enhances our performance and our wellbeing.

By having the "right" mindset, we're able to enter the magical state of flow. Although there's nothing magic about it. Not really. It certainly feels magical when you're in flow, but tapping into and maintaining it is within your control. All you need are some strategies and performance hacks to help you on your way.

When we can do this, we're on our way to becoming our own version of *Unashamedly Superhuman.* We can have increased confidence and improved mental focus if we simply structure our thinking in the right way.

But where do you start? How do you even restructure your thinking? What does that really mean? Well, it all starts with leaning into situations and learning how to use stress for good (contrary to popular belief, stress has many benefits in the right context). Don't believe me? Chapter 9 will change your mind.

Let's dive in because it turns out mind control might not just be reserved for superheroes after all. . . .

Chapter 9

LEAN IN

After a long, soul-destroying week of rejection, my sales manager would often try to motivate me with a rousing pep talk. "Come on, Jim," he'd say. "Make one more call. Finish the week on a high." Of course his encouragement was well-intentioned and although I appreciated the sentiment, sadly, it wasn't always enough to lift me out of my failure-induced downer. It was at that point that he'd pull out the big gun. I must have heard it a thousand times. In a pseudo-American drawl that resembled JR from the then hit TV show *Dallas*, he'd punch home the killer line: "C'MON, JIM, BE POSITIVE."

It's a killer line because you can't argue with it. You can't reply, NO! What I wanted to say was, I know, be positive. I want to be positive. I'm just not feeling very positive!

Do you know what I mean? Do you ever get those days when you think, "I've earned this depression and I'm going to have it!" In that moment the last thing you need is someone saying, "come on, be positive." You don't need a strapline, you need a strategy.

Mindsetting

Ever wonder what people mean when they say *mindset?* The definition I like most is: a word used to describe the way in which we lean into any given situation. *Mindsets* are defined as "the assumptions that you make about a particular thing." We have mindsets about many things: about food, exercise, and sleep, all of which we'll be taking a look at in Part IV, "Tapping into Physiology." Mindsets about yourself, your intelligence, and your abilities; mindsets about other people, their values, or their intentions. Mindsets about the world in general: Is it full of snakes or ladders? For now, how about we start where we left off in the last section of the book. What's your mindset about change; in particular, how do you feel about the stress that comes with it?

I mentioned briefly the impact of mindful reframing, and how the University of Wisconsin found that individuals who experienced a high level of stress throughout their life, but viewed stress as a trigger for growth and development, had dramatically lower rates of illness than individuals who experienced less stress, but viewed it as a bad thing. Let's expand that further and look at how we can view stress in ways that serve us better, as opposed to harming our physical performance and our mental well-being.

In general, do you view stress as good for you, or do you view it as debilitating and bad for you? Hold that thought for a moment. When looking into the nature of stress a couple of things became clear. One was that the public health message was consistent. Stress is bad: harmful to our health, our productivity, our relationships, our fertility, our cognition, you name it. The messages that were out there, by and large, focused on the damaging consequences of stress. But if you dive deeper into the literature and the origins of stress, what you find is it's not so clear-cut.

In fact, there's a large amount of evidence to support the fact that the experience of stress, meaning encountering adversity or challenge in our goal-related efforts, does not have to be debilitating and, in many cases, the body's response was designed to enhance our ability to manage those moments. The research shows that stress narrows our focus, increases our attention, and speeds up the rate at which we're able to process information. There was some research out there showing this phenomenon of physiological toughening. The process by which the stress response helps us to build our muscles, and build our neurons to help us grow and learn. Even the experience of the most traumatic stressors, the most chronic and enduring stressors, could lead not to distraction but, in fact, to the exact opposite: to an enhanced sense of connection with our values, connection to the sense of joy and passion for living.

I'm not trying to argue that stress is enhancing or debilitating, only to point out that the true nature of stress is a paradox. It's complex and lots of things can happen. So, what's the role of our mindset in shaping our response to stress?

Perception of the stressor

Do you view a stressor like a challenging exam or a health diagnosis or a demanding work schedule as a challenge or a threat? It's been shown, pretty convincingly, that when you view stressors less as a threat and more as a challenge, or an integral part of the adventure, your brain and body respond more adaptively. Dr Alia Crum from Stanford University[1] designed a measure to test people's mindsets about stress. She asked questions like: To what extent do you agree or disagree with statements like "Stress enhances my performance and productivity," "Stress heightens my vitality and growth?" She found, in a number of correlational studies, that a more enhancing stress mindset was linked to better health outcomes, better well-being, and higher performance. She then set out to see if it was possible to change people's mindsets.

Films were used that showcased facts about stress, but oriented towards one mindset or the other. One set of films reinforced the message depicting stress as a bad thing, the other films showed stress as a provocation to activate an optimum response. For example, images of basketball's LeBron James missing a vital free throw in the final minute versus one of him making it. So, either people saw a video that basically made it seem like stress will diminish you, crush you, and reduce you; or they watched a video which suggested stress will grow you and bring out your best, or maybe even take you to heightened levels of performance that you've never experienced before. It's much the same in terms of how leaders emerge in moments of greatest stress. Winston Churchill springs to mind, or in the United Kingdom at the onset of the COVID-19 pandemic the National Health Service asked for volunteers to step up and help. Overnight, half a million people applied! Examples are out there for both the enhancing nature and the debilitating nature of stress. The big question was: Does orienting people to different mindsets change how they respond?

[1] Crum, A. J., Salovey, P., and Achor, S., (2013), "Rethinking Stress: The Role of Mindsets in Determining the Stress Response," *Journal of Personality and Social Psychology*, 104(4): 716–733.

Crum et al. ran a study in the wake of the 2008 financial crisis, working with UBS, a financial services company that was undergoing massive amounts of layoffs. It was a tough time when employees were worried about their future. They set up three different conditions:

1. Some people watched no videos.
2. Some watched the "stress will crush you" videos.
3. Others watched the "stress could enhance you" videos.

Employees watched nine minutes of videos over the course of the week, which led to changes in their mindset and their physiological symptoms. People who watched the enhancing films had fewer backaches, muscle tension, insomnia, racing heart, and so forth. They also reported performing better at work compared to those who watch the debilitating videos. Interestingly, the debilitating videos didn't make anyone worse. They concluded that responding to negative messages is nothing new. What was inspiring was the positive impact of focusing on this enhancing perspective.

When you broaden the discussion to how we go through our lives responding to the many challenges and opportunities, it appears there are essentially three positions we can take: back on our heels, flat-footed, or leaning in/forward.

Leaning in

The hack here focuses on leaning into stressful situations, otherwise known as our adventure. It's important to understand that any time we're challenging ourselves, we're going to have adrenaline in our bodies. The question is, will it be mixed with too much cortisol, which can set us back on our heels, or with dopamine, which will drive us forward? We talked about the fact that adrenaline's major role is to place us into a moment with a focus on action. We also looked at some hacks that enable us to reduce the amount of adrenaline with dopamine, enabling us to suppress the quit reflex.

This is a compelling example of how simply changing our mindset around stress can help. I've never worked with the Navy SEALS (the U.S. special forces), but Dr Crum has.

So, at the beginning of their training programme, the recruits completed a questionnaire that revealed whether or not they had a stress-enhancing mindset or a stress-debilitating mindset. Then researchers looked at how well recruits performed during that programme. On average, only 15 percent get through with a pass. What researchers found was, based on the recruits' mindset (stress-enhancing or stress-debilitating), they could predict who would pass and who wouldn't.

Essentially, those with the stress-enhancing mindset were more likely to complete training and become a SEAL. They had faster obstacle course times and they were rated by their peers more positively. Let's be clear, this doesn't mean you should like stress. Well, maybe the SEALs do, but that's not what I'm saying. Having a stress-enhancing mindset doesn't mean the stressor is a good thing. It doesn't mean that getting a cancer diagnosis is a good thing or being in abject poverty is a good thing. These are not good things. But the experience of the stress associated with the adversity can lead to enhanced outcomes with respect to not just our cognition, but our health, our performance, and our well-being.

So, how does that work?

First, it fundamentally changes what we're motivated to do. If we're stressed about something in a bad way, like a global pandemic, for instance, what's your motivation? Not only do you have the pandemic to deal with, but you also have the stress about the pandemic. Second, your reaction is typically to do one of two things. It's either to freak out and do everything you can to make sure that this doesn't affect you or to check out and say, "It's not a big deal, I'm not going to deal with it." Basically, denial. People who have a stress-debilitating mindset tend to go to one or the other of those extremes: freak out or check out.

However, if you have a stress-enhancing mindset, the motivation changes to how do I utilise the stress to realise my outcomes?

What can we do to learn from this experience? How can it make us Better, Smarter, or Stronger?

So, how do we leverage it and utilise it?

Rather than define *stress* as only having negative consequences, the first step is to decouple that and to realise that stress is neutral. How we can do that is to understand that we only stress about things we care about, things that matter to us. We don't stress about things we don't care about. For example, if I said that Sandy lost their job that wouldn't stress you unless Sandy was your child or if you were Sandy. It only becomes stressful to the extent that you care about it. So, the key question here is why are we trying to fight or run away from or merely cope with things we care about?

Performance hack: Three steps to adopting a stress-enhancing mindset

Step 1: Acknowledge that you're stressed. See it and own it. Be mindful.

Step 2: Welcome it. Why would you do that? Here, you're using it as an opportunity to reconnect to what it is that you care about.

Step 3: Utilise the stress response to achieve the thing that you care about instead of spending your time, money, effort, and energy trying to get rid of the stress.

There is good news, so bear with me on this one. The physiological effects of stress that are most impressive are that it narrows visual attention, creating focus. It drives our capacity to deal with time moving quickly. Have you ever had a day where you're engrossed in a demanding piece of work and, before you know it, the day is over and you're wondering where the time went? That ability to deal with time moving quickly, in turn, drives our capacity to process information faster. It might feel uncomfortable, but acknowledging it, embracing it, and then understanding it is a tremendous focusing mechanism.

And here's the bonus, unlike the relaxation response that takes effort to achieve, we don't need any training to activate the stress response. It's built in; it's free. You could call it a superpower!

Cast your mind back to a time when you were channeling your inner superhuman. *Being in the zone* is the phrase typically used. There are other terms used to describe this super productive state of consciousness: *athlete's high, on a roll, automatic,* or simply, *having a blinder.* Let's call it *flow.*

Where were you, what were you doing? Skiing down a black run or pulling together a complex project plan? Deeply engrossed in a riveting conversation with friends or banging out a tune on your instrument of choice? As you reflect back, how would you describe your experience?

When I ask people, answers typically include:

- "Everything felt effortless."
- "All of my skills showed up when it mattered."
- "Complete concentration."
- "It was fully immersive and nothing could distract me."
- "Merger of action and awareness."
- "I felt totally in the moment. I was able to make fast decisions, sometimes without even thinking."
- "A sense of control."
- "Sounds fell away and every action and every decision led seamlessly, fluidly to the next step."
- "Time distortion."
- "Sometimes it slowed down and I felt like I had all the time in the world. Other times an hour felt more like five minutes."

This tunnel-vision phenomenon is reported by athletes, creatives, and psychologists alike as a hyper-focused state of mind where anything is possible, where we both feel and perform at our best. It's where we become our most productive, creative, and powerful selves. Pattern recognition, future prediction, information processing, these skills are massively amplified. Flow heightens intellectual performance, heightens creative performance, and heightens physical performance.

Mihaly Csikszentmihalyi was a Hungarian-American psychologist and Professor of Psychology and Management at Claremont Graduate University. He was known affectionately as the "godfather of flow." He defined *flow* as "a time where we are completely involved in an activity for its own sake. The ego falls away. Time flies. Every action, movement and thought follows inevitably from the previous one, like playing jazz. Your whole being is involved, and you're using your skills to the utmost."[2]

The many advantages of flow include an uplift in motivation and productivity, learning and memory, creativity and innovation, grit and persistence, empathy, and collaboration and cooperation. A study carried out by McKinsey[3] stated, "When we ask executives how much more productive they were at their peak performance than they were on average, the comment at senior levels is an increase of five times."

Forbes magazine[4] noted, "The number one management metric you need to know? Flow state percentage. Interruptions that move us out of a flow state increase R&D cycle times and costs dramatically."

FaST CoMPANY[5] put it like this. "Major companies, including Microsoft, Ericsson, Patagonia and Toyota, have realised that being able to control and harness this feeling of flow is the holy grail for any manager."

The recurring theme is clear: from runner's high to third eye, when we drop into flow, we feel powerful and purposeful and we are more able to tap into our very best selves. So, it would appear that everyone has tapped into flow at some point in their lives. The million-dollar question then is: We've been there, but how the hell do we get back? At two o'clock tomorrow afternoon

---

[2] Csikszentmihalyi, M., (2008), *Flow: The Psychology of Optimal Experience*, Ingram International Inc.

[3] Cranston, S., and Keller, S., (2013), "Increasing the 'Meaning Quotient' of Work," *McKinsey & Company*, 1 January. Available at: https://www.mckinsey.com/business-functions/people-and-organizational-performance/our-insights/increasing-the-meaning-quotient-of-work.

[4] Upbin, B., (2011), "Five New Management Metrics You Need To Know," *Forbes*, 13 December. Available at: https://www.forbes.com/sites/bruceupbin/2011/12/13/five-new-management-metrics-you-need-to-know/?sh=a0b0384717d4.

[5] Marsh, A., (2005), "The Art of Work," *FaST CoMPANY*, 1 August. Available at: https://www.fastcompany.com/53713/art-work.

you're delivering that mission-critical pitch, have that long awaited audition or interview, or you're due off the first tee. What has to happen in order to tap into that all-too-often elusive state of flow?

Getting high on your own supply

What if there was a special pill out there that you could take once a day that would suddenly allow you to tap into all your brain's potential? What if you were able to recall everything you had ever learned, every language you had ever studied, and every fight move you ever watched? How would your life change if you were able to fully actualize your abilities to your full potential, both physically and mentally? Now, you may think of these as silly questions, but the film *Limitless*, starring Bradley Cooper, explores these in an entertaining and thought-provoking manner. Instead of working hard, taking risks, and pushing ourselves to be better people, *Limitless* proposes a fictional scenario where a special pill, taken just once a day, can make all the difference. You don't have to do any heavy lifting as the pill you take will unlock all your hidden potential allowing you to be free to pursue your dreams and goals. Sounds too good to be true, doesn't it? Well, *Limitless* lets the audience decide if this illustrious pill is worth the risk involved and whether you would even truly need a pill to become the best version of yourself.

In case you haven't seen it, the movie goes a bit like this. Facing unemployment and his girlfriend's rejection, writer Eddie Morra (Bradley Cooper) is sure that he has no future. That all changes when an old friend gives him a drug that produces enhanced mental acuity. Stoked on the untested chemical, Eddie rises to the top of the financial world and attracts the attention of a tycoon (Robert De Niro) who intends to use him to make a fortune. But terrible side-effects and a dwindling supply threaten to collapse Eddie's house of cards. What's that, terrible side effects? Actually, even with the side effects, it still seems like a compelling option. However, it's fictional, at the moment at least.

I introduce *Limitless* purely as a provocative metaphor for potentiality, but instead of pill-popping our way to a supercharged mind/body connection, I'd like to offer an equally potent, but less fanciful, way of propelling us cognitively and physically to another level of performance.

In the first part of *Unashamedly Superhuman*, "BETTER—Tapping into Potential," we look at how we can adapt better to endure less when navigating life's challenges and opportunities. An integral part are the *performance hacks* that enable us to maintain forward motion by provoking a dopamine release in order to buffer the adrenaline-fuelled stress response, keeping the quit reflex at bay. It's important here to say that adrenaline isn't necessarily a bad thing. In the right dose and when it's combined with the right cocktail of brain chemistry, it's an energising component of this highly prized flow state. Thanks to modern neuroscience, we now understand flow states are induced via interactions between five different neurotransmitters:

1. Dopamine – shows up when you want something. Focus and motivation.
2. Norepinephrine – along with dopamine, tightens your focus.
3. Endorphins – block pain, allowing you to work longer.
4. Anandamide – prompts lateral mental connections. Encourages insights.
5. Serotonin – the "feel good" chemical.

When you enter into flow, *dopamine* floods the brain. It increases attention, information flow, and pattern recognition. It acts as a skill booster. It has what's known as a long arc, meaning the boost is long-lasting and slow to diminish. Some scientists say it's Mother Nature's cocaine. All the energy but without the crash and burn. *Norepinephrine* (aka adrenaline) speeds up the heart rate, muscle tension, and respiration. It triggers a glucose response so we have more energy, increasing attention, neural efficiency, and emotional control. The nearest external provider might be Adderall. A rush of adrenaline can be experienced as a high. Adrenaline junkies know the feeling. *Endorphins* are next. The word *endorphine* derives from the word *endogenous,* meaning "naturally internal to the body." Endorphins relieve pain and induce pleasure. *Anandamide* stems from the Sanskrit word for *bliss.* It is an endogenous cannabinoid and feels similar to the psychoactive effect found in marijuana. Anandemide is released in exercise-induced flow states, elevates mood, relieves pain, dilates blood vessels, and aids respiration. It has also been proven to amplify lateral thinking. At the end of the flow state, *serotonin* fills the brain, producing an afterglow effect. It occurs after the flow state has been and gone.

In a nutshell, these five chemicals make up the brain science of flow states. A potent combination proven to contribute to overall performance, happiness, and well-being. Flow is the only state that releases all five of these chemicals at once. That's why flow states can produce the most powerful motivation on the planet.

Researchers describe flow as the source code of intrinsic motivation. Everything we're going to look at in this section of *Unashamedly Superhuman* can be summed up in just one word: **Focus**. The golden rule is: *flow follows focus.*

Chapter 10

FLOW FOLLOWS FOCUS

Steven Kotler is regarded by many, myself included, as the world's leading authority on all things flow-related. He is a multi-award–winning author and heads up a group of neuroscientists and performance psychologists at the Flow Research Collective. If you want a full immersion into the subject, he runs a phenomenal programme called *Zero to Dangerous.* He asks a great question: "How the hell do you know if you're in flow?"

He talks about how the research of Mihaly Csikszentmihalyi, and a few other scientists, uncovered 10 core characteristics that underpin the state. Interestingly, he points out that while each of these phenomena can be experienced independently, when they all show up together—that's flow. The research his group has done suggests that the first six of these characteristics constitute flow, whereas the last four (intense concentration, immediate feedback, clear goals, and the challenge/skills ratio) are characteristics of the state. He goes on to say that these four are what they call "flow triggers" or preconditions that lead to the experience. It's not that these "characteristics" aren't present during the state, it's more that they tend to arise before the state itself and are drivers that propel us into it. So, to sum up, we talked earlier about our experience of flow, but you might find the following list to be useful if you want to know if an experience qualifies as flow.

1. *Action and Awareness Merge:* The doer and the doing become one. From the perspective of consciousness, we become the action. In other words, actions feel automatic and require little or no additional resources.
2. *Selflessness:* Our sense of self disappears. Our sense of self-consciousness as well. The inner critic is silenced.
3. *Timelessness:* We experience an altered perception of time. Past and future disappear, and we are plunged into an eternal present, a deep now.
4. *Effortlessness:* Our sense of struggle and strife vanishes. The experience becomes intrinsically rewarding or in technical parlance autotelic.

5. *Paradox of Control:* We have a powerful sense of control over the situation. We are captain of our own ship, master of this small slice of destiny.

6. *Intrinsic Motivation:* The experience is intrinsically motivating. We do it for love not money. We do it because the activity itself is so incredibly enthralling that it is its own reward.

7. *Intense Concentration:* More specifically, intense concentration on a limited field of information. Total focus on the right here, right now. Complete absorption in the present moment.

8. *Clear Goals:* These are not big goals, like winning that promotion, rather they are much smaller chunks, like completing your CV or preparing for the interview. What's critical is we know what we're doing now and we know what we're doing next, so our attention can stay focused in the present.

9. *Immediate Feedback:* The gap between cause and effect is tiny—so we can always course-correct mid-flight.

10. *Challenge/Skills Balance:* The challenge of the task at hand slightly exceeds our skill set so we have to push ourselves outside our comfort zone. But not too far outside.

Along with neurochemistry, flow triggers help you to reduce cognitive load. Reduce what your brain is paying attention to, and more mental energy is freed up to power the thing you're trying to do. Think about what gets you excited, energised, engaged, and curious. Those are the things that hold your flow triggers.

Stretch but don't snap

You may have noticed that the price of bicycles went through the roof during the first lockdown. In the United Kingdom, we were limited to an hour's exercise per day and people wanted to take every opportunity to get out and about. For the first time in our lives, there were more bikes on the roads than there were cars. It was wonderful. If that was you too, you'll remember how safe you felt. Free and easy riding. No risk, no danger, no traffic to consider, and certainly no need to be super focused. No need for flow. Compare that to riding through the streets of London now. Now your brain reacts in a very different way. In order to rise to the challenge of navigating the cut and thrust of rush-hour traffic, your brain flips the switch and pumps in some of the aforementioned chemicals enabling you to raise your game. The chemicals were always there, but they are only released on a need-to-have basis. The extra demand is the trigger. This is known as the skills challenge balance.

If you're a skier, you'll be familiar with the chart that denotes ski run codes in different countries. For example, beginner runs are denoted by green circles in North America and Japan, or by blue circles in Europe. Intermediate runs, meanwhile, are a blue square in North America, and red circles in Europe and Japan. Expert runs (black runs) are universally the same colour, but denoted by a diamond in North America and circles in Europe and Japan. North America also has symbols for "Expert only" and "Terrain park" but let's not get too bogged down in the details.

You'll also know that the purpose of the colour coding is to enable you to establish the perfect skills/challenge match. The perfect match for triggering flow would be the one that takes you to the edge of your skill level. What happens to a black-run skier on a green slope? No stretch, no flow. No flow necessary, no flow triggered. How about a green-run skier on a black run? Even if you were in flow on an easy section of the slope as soon as the skills/challenge balance tips too far where the challenge outweighs the current skill level, we get spit out of flow. Typically this is preceded by an over-fixation on the scale of the problem, resulting in you losing your edge, flipping onto your back, and bouncing down the mountain you had no business being on.

Putting the triggers into action: My IRONMAN® event and flow

At the time, I was certainly no expert in how to apply flow to sport. I'd tried hard to force the issue during training runs, and although there is no doubt on reflection I'd wafted in and out of what I now know to be "the zone," I didn't have it down to a dependable art form. I'd been advised when swimming to allow my focus to take in more peripheral visual information, notice the riverbank or a distant tree line whilst taking a breath to the side. It seemed to provide entry to a productive rhythm. Was it flow? I'm not sure, although time passed and muscles relaxed, so maybe in part. During the first 10 to 20 minutes on a run, where I was trying to convince myself that two or three hours pounding the pavement in the rain was a good idea, I was advised to focus on how good it feels to run with good form whilst regulating my breathing. Because I run barefoot, my stride cadence is 170 per minute, syncing that to my breathing also helped focus my attention on form. Did it produce flow? I'm not sure, although with the accompanying music it was pleasantly hypnotic, so somewhat. However, on my big day, from the moment I popped on my swimming goggles, started my stopwatch, and kicked off in the lake to start the 2.4-mile (3.9-km) swim leg, and for the following 12 and a half hours, I most certainly was. To one degree or another, whether mild or deep, I was in the zone all day long. It wasn't a surprise to me. I expected it to happen because I planned for it to happen. You can examine the external and internal flow trigger checklists that follow to see if any or all are connected to the situation or environment where flow would provide the high performance and well-being boost that you're looking for. As I reflect on my day-long IRONMAN® race adventure, to a lesser or greater degree, I recognise them all.

External triggers

High consequence? Many people shared their concern that I may push myself too hard at the expense of my own health. Was my body up to the job? I genuinely had no idea. My longest training session had been half the distance two months prior. Also, as I was going solo, if I crashed and burned there were no paramedics on hand with a magic sponge. Joking aside, I had my concerns up until the moment I got in the water, after that it never crossed my mind.

Novelty? Safe to say I'd never experienced anything like this before! New experiences. New challenges. New emotions. New achievements.

Complexity? I wasn't sure about this one until I reflected afterwards. However, my nutritional strategy involved an element of complexity that I wasn't used to. They often say that nutrition is the fourth discipline in a triathlon. Eating too much or not enough, based on body weight and effort level, can bring you down in the later stages. Fail to take on the right amount of liquids and electrolytes at the right frequency throughout the day, based on body weight and your propensity to sweat, and you'll dehydrate. You won't just crash and burn, the likelihood is the hallucinogenic state you'll be in will end your race. Images of Bambi learning to walk come to mind.

Unpredictability? All of the above. Not to mention the weather, cars on the road, and possible mechanical, physical, or mental breakdowns.

Deep embodiment? Every cell in my body was fully invested in this day. I didn't listen to the news before leaving the house at 5 a.m. Phone off. No emails or social media checked. Every thought, decision, and action was directed towards being in the moment and staying there as best I could for as long as I could.

Internal triggers

Clear goals? My end goal and performance goals were clear. End goals: 90-minute swim, six-hour bike, four-hour run, 60 minutes of transition and feeding stops spread throughout the day. I didn't hit them all exactly, but it was close enough. Performance goals: Remain calm and alert; focus on breathing and form; regularly self-reward with encouragement and appreciation for having the opportunity to test myself; eat and drink the planned amount—breakfast at 4 a.m. and during transitions, then every 30 minutes on the bike and every 45 minutes on the run.

Unambiguous feedback? Physically and emotionally I was processing feedback constantly. How was I feeling? Was I getting stronger or weaker? Should I step it up a bit or ease back? How were the energy levels? Was the nutrition kicking in? What was my heart rate? Was it sustainable? Externally, I'd arranged to be tracked by a group of family and friends on a tracking app. From start to finish they could see where I was on the course, my pace, whether I'd stopped for a break and when I was close to home to transition off the bike. It added dynamic tension. Nobody was going to judge me more than I'd judge myself, but it felt good knowing my efforts were being monitored. It kept me moving during some of the times when I felt like stopping. It helped me suppress the quit reflex.

Challenge/skill balance? When I originally came up with the idea the skills/challenge balance was way out of whack. Huge challenge, little to no relevant skills. But that was three years prior. I still didn't know for sure if I'd bitten off more than I could chew, but I did know that I'd trained hard and I trusted my strategy. I also had a belief system that I wouldn't have been able to conceive the idea in the first place and set the goal, unless at some level it was possible. That belief drove my preparation, which put me in the best possible position to achieve it. Of course, that could have all been delusional, but it made sense at the time, and turned out to be true on this occasion.

Concentration on the task? Concentration bordering on obsession. From swim stroke to food consumption. From bike balance to run cadence. From breathwork to energy management I don't think I could have been more focused on the task at hand.

Curiosity? That's an interesting one. I was certainly curious to see how I would respond to the demands that this day would put on me. More so, however, I couldn't wait to see if some of my unusual training methods had worked. I knew I'd dig deep and push myself but after the numerous surgeries on my knees and back would I hold up structurally? Specifically, there were three things that I'd done every day, religiously over the previous 24 months that I'd never even heard of before: First, a 30-minute breathwork practice, and second, a 10-minute cold shower, both designed to strengthen the respiratory and cardiovascular systems, and regulate the stress response. The third was the decision to transition from comfy cushioned running shoes in favour of running barefoot. I was blown away by the results. More on that during the final section of *Unashamedly Superhuman*, Tapping into Physiology.

Passion? I can't claim to have a passion for any of the three component parts of triathlon. Nor for keeping fit in general. Like many people I have a love-hate relationship with exercise. I always feel better afterwards, but need a burning platform in order to take it seriously. However, I am passionate about learning how to combine high performance with well-being. I'm inspired when working with people who are exploring their limits and tapping into their potential. Those associations generated enough passion to drive me on the day.

Purpose? When we're driven by a purpose, we don't just know *what* we want, we know *why* we want it. Furthermore, the *why* is so big it makes finding a *how* almost inevitable. I certainly knew why I was taking on this challenge. I was endeavouring to find out how to harness inner power to achieve our greatest personal and professional goals. It had a ring to it.

Autonomy? Autonomy is the need to direct your own life and work. To be fully motivated, you must be able to control what you do, when you do it, and whom you do it with. As one of the characteristics of intrinsic motivation (motivation from the inside out), taking ownership of every aspect of the day was fundamental. I decided at the start that no matter what happened externally, it was all part of the experience and I would value it. The weather, traffic, punctures, injuries, everything. As it happens, it couldn't have gone more smoothly, no drama. It might have been interesting to see how I would have responded under duress. Would I have maintained such a philosophical perspective whilst sitting on the side of the road in the rain trying to change a tyre a mile from home with a marathon still to run? Let's just say I lucked out!

Bonus trigger? This bonus trigger doesn't appear in any of the literature that I read during my two-year dive into the mystery of flow states, but I think it should be. It's the desire to prove something or someone wrong. It wasn't my primary driver and I wasn't even aware of it until deep into the marathon. It was at the point where I knew I was going to finish the IRONMAN® triathlon. I had a flashback to 2004. I was walking out of the hospital having had my final consultation following the surgery that fused two discs at the base of my back. Although I was grateful that the operation was a success, the well-intentioned surgeon had just told me there was nothing more that could be done to address my chronic back pain and that my most active days were now behind me. No more running. No more anything that might undo the spinal reconstruction. I was 40 years old, and the impact it had on my self-worth and self-confidence was significant. I remember trying to ready myself for the inevitable decline that lay ahead. Fast forward to mile 24 (39 km) on 2 September 2021. I practically floated through the final couple of miles of the 140 (225 km) covered that day, meditating on this additional flow trigger. It dawned on me that I wasn't trying to prove him wrong, I was elated because I'd proven my own limiting beliefs to be wrong. Very wrong.

Chapter 11

ONE, TWO, THREE MINDS

I wondered how many books have been published on positive thinking? Intuitively I figured the answer would be somewhere in the region of quite a lot. One result from my Google search stated that unit sales of self-help books have grown at a compound annual growth rate of 11 percent in six years, reaching 18.6 million in 2019.[1] It's a huge market. One book alone, Norman Vincent Peale's *The Power of Positive Thinking*[2] has sold millions of copies worldwide.

My introduction to this self-help genre came in 1984 when I started an eight-year career with the Combined Insurance Company of America. The founder and CEO at the time was self-made millionaire W. Clement Stone. In 1959, he teamed up with another giant of positive thinking, author Napoleon Hill, and the result was *Success Through a Positive Mental Attitude*,[3] the phenomenon that proposed to the world that with the right attitude, anyone can achieve his or her dreams.

This bestselling self-help classic promoted positive mental attitude as a key to personal success. It states that your mind has a secret invisible talisman. On one side is emblazoned the letters PMA (positive mental attitude) and on the other the letters NMA (negative mental attitude). The central message of the book is that a positive attitude will naturally attract the good and the beautiful. The negative attitude will rob you of all that makes life worth living. Your success, health, happiness, and wealth depend on how you make up your mind! Personally I think there is a bit more to it than that; however, it's probably fair to say that, delusion aside, positive beats negative hands down. Whichever way you look at it, positive thinking is in and

---

[1] Pierce, D., (2021), "Self-Help Books Fill a Burgeoning Need," *Library Journal*, 9 March. Available at: https://www.libraryjournal.com/story/self-help-books-fill-a-burgeoning-need.
[2] Peale, N.V., (1990), *The Power of Positive Thinking*, Cedar Books/Vermilion, New edition.
[3] Hill, N., and Stone, W.C., (1997), *Success Through a Positive Mental Attitude: Discover the Secret of Making Your Dreams Come True*, Thorsons, New edition.

of itself a huge topic and worthy of an entire book. I'm only giving it one chapter. So I need to be specific about my angle and it has nothing to do with BELIEVE AND SUCCEED!

My interest is the impact our mindset has on our ability to tap into flow. We've looked at a list of 14 flow triggers, five external and nine internal, each of which can nudge us into the direction of that super productive state of mind. At the same time, it's equally vital to understand that there are four flow blockers. Distractions, interruptions, and fatigue can all make flow extremely difficult to access but most important of all is the number one flow blocker, negativity. It's a barrier to entry.

My observation then, is there are not one, not two, but three minds. Negative mind, positive mind, and flow mind, and you can't get to flow mind from negative mind.

The single point of focus for this chapter is how we can hang out more often in positive mind in order to have easier access to flow mind. Not easy at the best of times because it will typically require us to challenge what we believe to be true or what we believe to be possible.

I first saw it in Shanghai. . . .

It was at the end of a long day. A conference for 1,000 or so enthusiastic pharmaceuticals sales representatives was coming to a close. It was time for the finale. The Shaolin monks were about to mesmerise us with an extraordinary demonstration of acrobatics and martial arts. A blur of orange robes flying and flailing across the stage. A full half-hour of derring-do. Supreme fitness and remarkable feats of mind over matter followed. Wooden boards were smashed karate-style, endless somersaults, and an equal amount of what I think are called Arab-springs. Then it happened: the finale to the finale.

The spotlight shone across the dimmed stage and settled on a man who I would later find out to be a Grandmaster. He was 80 if he was a day, and he practically floated to centre-stage. He stopped, and with an audible exhale, summoned his *chi*.

The room was silent. Again the spotlight darted back stage left, to reveal one of the lesser Shaolins, a helper. An apprentice master perhaps. My age group would call him *Grasshopper*. He moved less elegantly towards the Grandmaster sporting a quiver of arrows on his back. With a sudden movement he whipped out an arrow, sprung into a martial arts stance, legs bent at the knee, sideways to his opponent, both arms stretched out straight in front holding the arrow by the feathered end. The tip of the arrow, to the surprise of everyone, had come to rest directly in front of the Grandmaster's throat. Everyone's surprise, that is, except the Grandmaster's. He didn't even blink! He did, however, turn his head to face his assailant, causing the sharp metal tip to sink into what is technically termed the *suprasternal notch, jugular notch*, or arrow socket!

Without so much as a pause, the orange-clad ninja lurched towards his opponent instantly snapping the arrow with his bare throat! My initial thought was, unsurprisingly, "WHY? Why would you do that?"

The crowd, however, erupted. Applause filled the conference centre. My thoughts turned quickly to, "You can't argue with results, Jim. As a conference close, that is clearly a winner!"

I'm a professional speaker. I could use that. Surely I could somehow crowbar an arrow snap in whenever I wanted to challenge people to step outside their comfort zones. Everything we know about arrows tells us they go *into things*! Who's going to want to snap one with their own throat? It's ridiculous, but what a great metaphor, and better than that, it's entertaining! I had to find out how to do it.

I stayed behind after the event to speak to the organiser. I asked if he could arrange for me to speak to the Grandmaster and 30 minutes later he returned with a Chinese lady. She introduced herself, in perfect English, as the head of PR for the Shaolin monks, and informed me that her office was in Baker Street in London! Who knew?

I explained how impressed I'd been by the show, and that I'd particularly like to speak to the monk with the arrow. "What for?" she asked curiously. "I'd like to give it a go" I said innocently.

"But he's a Grandmaster," she explained. "He's spent many years training himself to achieve such a feat of *chi management!*" or something.

"No," I said, "It was good, but. . ." I went on to explain that I'd long held the belief that given similar resources, and similar skills, you can get similar results as the next person. I reasoned that I have a throat (the necessary resource) and, stepping forward, one foot planting itself 3 feet in front of the other in the same way that I'd seen in the demonstration on stage, I clearly had the necessary skill.

"All I'm lacking is the arrow," I said confidently. I assumed it was a specific arrow, and for health and safety thought prudent to get the make and model. For all I cared it could have been made of balsa wood, or half sawn through the middle. . . I just wanted the strategy that would enable me to become an arrow-snapper! The PR lady didn't take kindly to the *sawn through the middle* suggestion.

"Of course it isn't!" she spat. Excellent, I thought, I can allow the audience to check the arrow first, even better. Now, it wasn't my intention to insult the Shaolin tradition by suggesting that a mere mortal could, with no training in chi management, "*do the arrow*," but she didn't take kindly to the inference. Needless to say, I didn't get to meet the Grandmaster and I left with no arrows.

On my return to London, I told my bizarre tale to the proprietor at a sports shop, insisting that the arrow seemed to break easily. He suggested they weren't competition arrows but more likely practice arrows, made of wood with a 15lb breaking strain. They came in boxes of 50 that were duly ordered and shortly after arrived at my office. A small group of us gathered. Open-neck shirts replaced orange gowns and a mixture of curious enthusiasm, adrenalin and terror replaced chi. A wedge of protective paper towels on the throat prompted the "courage" to get us started.

First arrow, snapped. Paper towel inspection—not too much damage.

Second arrow with reduced paper towel protection—snapped.

Gradually, sheet by sheet, the protection was whittled down. Finally, after several tense hours of activity, we were snapping arrows, just like the Grandmaster, directly on our throats.

Since then, I've used this demonstration many times, having a *volunteer* come on stage to demonstrate what it takes to overcome the negative assumption that the arrow will cause them physical harm. As intended, it does indeed demonstrate that if we have similar resources and similar skills, we can get similar results as the next person. It's also a powerful metaphor, to demonstrate the *power of the mind*. But that's not the reason I use it. The *intention* isn't to show that "anything is possible" or some other such West Coast motivational mantra. The punch line is simply this: Snapping an arrow on your throat is easy. The volunteer realises it the moment they step towards it. The audience realises it too. Snapping the arrow isn't difficult. It never was. Getting on stage to find out is. It's always easy getting a second volunteer. So, what changes? They haven't changed, the arrow hasn't changed, but having seen the first volunteer leave the stage triumphantly, they have moved from negative mind to positive mind. Now they are able to break out of their comfort zone, kick into action, and step into flow.

Negative mind is typically associated with things like self-criticism, worry, and doubt. Positive mind is linked to possibility, a can-do approach, and flow. This is sometimes called no mind, on account that we're less aware of our actual thoughts, and is when we're *doing* more than we're *thinking*.

Negative mind is an understandable and sometimes appropriate reaction to demanding and difficult situations. Concern and doubt are perhaps our mind's way of steering us away from complacency. However, if those patterns of thought remain unchecked they can lead to anxiety and make it difficult to gain access to our most productive problem solving capabilities. In this context, when I refer to a positive mind, I just mean the content of our thinking is such that it's typically optimistic, a place that creates space. Negative mind puts us on the back foot whilst a positive mind enables us to see a way forward, and when I say *see* a way forward, I mean that quite literally. Negativity can cause something known as a *scotoma,* a blind spot.

How to shift from negative mind to positive mind?

Have you ever lost your car keys? Me too, many times. When you lose your keys do you have a circuit you go on? Kitchen, lounge, table by the door, jackets hanging in the hallway? If after the first lap of the circuit you haven't found them then what do you do? Do you ever go round again? After four more laps of the circuit and 20 exasperating minutes, has your partner or someone else in your house ever said, "What are these?" as they pick them up off a table that you know you've walked past at least five times? "You walk around with your eyes closed," is a phrase I've heard more times than I care to remember. Obviously that's not literally the case, but we might as well be. Let me explain what's happening. As soon as we say to ourselves, "I've lost my keys," our brain responds by saying something along the lines of, "OK, you seem pretty sure about that, I'll see what I can do!" Its job now is to prove you right. So even though your eyes see the keys on the first lap, it's like your hands are waving in front of your eyes stopping you from seeing what's right in front of you, and off you go on the next circuit. Three laps later and your eyes are going crazy, "THERE ARE THE KEYS, THERE

ARE THE KEYS," but your brain's got a job to do and it replies "They said they can't find them, don't make them out to be a liar!" Another lap!

Now, if you're reading this thinking, I never lose my keys, the reason is your internal dialogue and focus is simply more conducive to the task at hand. You don't say, "I've lost my keys," which provokes the scotoma, the blind spot that blocks them out of our conscious vision, instead you say something like, "Where are my keys?" causing you to call to mind a mental image of your keys. In the same way buying a grey Audi causes us to see more grey Audis, visualising the keys primes our mind to notice things that align with that thought. It's not that I have a negative attitude and you a positive one, but our inner voice is nudging us to either negative mind or positive mind. We're both looking for our keys, but the difference is I'm hot and bothered and running around like a headless chicken whilst you're off and out and getting on with your day.

Performance hack: Positive priming questions

Priming questions are designed to pull something to the front of your mind. When you prime your mind to focus on a particular thought or idea, your brain adapts to process related information more readily. Use these priming questions at the start of your day, to set you up for what's ahead. By taking just a few minutes to answer these questions, you'll reduce the cognitive load your brain has to process over the course of the day.

Take out a pen a paper and as you ask yourself the following. As you write down your answers to these three simple questions, take a moment to visualise the situation you're focusing on and think about how that will apply to your day. The first question is: "What am I going to let go of today?" For example, imagine you have a big presentation coming up. The answer could be, "I'm going to let go of tension and nervousness, so that when I give my presentation, I remain calm and take my time." Sounds simple enough.

Whatever you decide you are going to let go of dwell on your answer for just a minute and create a mental movie of how your day would benefit if you did. Next consider the question: "What am I grateful for today?" Pause and focus on some of the positive attributes that you have that will lend themselves to the task ahead. Confidence, competence, composure, or courage, perhaps. It's not enough to simply pick out the words; it's important to feel them as you project ahead. You could also think of a previous time when you successfully demonstrated such attributes. Hold the thought momentarily and feel the feelings you felt in that past situation. Alternatively, you could experience a sense of gratitude by reframing the situation. Instead of thinking you *have* to do the presentation, decide that you *get* to do it. Somebody else could have received the opportunity to present, but they didn't, you did! This shifts the focus to the return on investment for your efforts.

Finally, ask yourself: "What am I definitely going to accomplish today?" Of all the things on your to-do list, write down the one or two most important items that without any doubt will get done.

You can then move on and go about your day. But now your mind is working on achieving that. You've also triggered a dopamine release that comes from setting off your seeking system (as I explained in Chapter 5). You're primed for what's coming.

1. What am I going to let go of today?
2. What am I grateful for today?
3. What am I definitely going to accomplish today?

Instead of asking what do I think about the day ahead, instead ask what do I need to think in order to shift from negative mind to positive mind?

Designer beliefs

I had my first pair of glasses sometime in my late 40s. Reading was still fine, but clarity at 66 feet (20 metres) or more was only possible after assuming a strained contortion resembling that of Derek Zoolander's *blue steel*.

A visit to the opticians soon took care of that. Short sighted-ness addressed, I took the opportunity to enquire about my only other eye issue. Since primary school I knew I had an issue with colours. Regularly mistaking greens for browns, browns for reds, and don't get me started on purples and a colour that I still couldn't pick out of an identity parade, the mystery that is mauve!

Once, on a business trip to Hong Kong, I took advantage of the made-to-measure service. 24 hours later three, three-piece suits arrived at my hotel: one dark brown, another a pale blue summer suit, and finally a natty, linen number in a light tan. My schoolboy excitement evaporated soon after arriving home. Not one, not two, but all three were a different shade of green. Even the lady at the charity shop just asked, "*Why*?!"

So, I wondered if my condition had a name? After a further test I was labelled "strong deutan." Although I am particularly "deutanous," it's not so rare in men, one in 12, in fact. Less so for females, only one in 200 women have the condition.

I wondered if either of my girls saw things like me? A quick visit to Google and I found two of the slides that the optician had used to assess me. On it are two circles, made up of multiple different sized (and coloured) dots. In the first circle, the number "25" is clearly visible, as it's made up of orange dots on a green background (well, it is if you're not a "strong deutan"!). When I showed this to my daughters and asked what number they saw, they both immediately said 25. You won't be surprised to hear that I too can see 25.

The second circle is trickier. For those who are not deutanous, the number "6" is visible, albeit a bit more challenging to make out in this circle than the "25" in the first one. The dots making up the "6" are a blend of greens, oranges, and browns, while the dots in the background are a mix of reds, oranges, and yellows.

On showing this to my daughters, I asked, "how about the circle on the right?" Without hesitation they both said, "six." "You can see a six?" "Uh, yeah, there," they pointed. "I can't see a six, or any number, just a pattern. It's called "Strong Deutan," I said proudly. "You can't see that number six? That six, there?" this time with incredulity. "Nope, no six." "What's the matter with you?" they enquired. "Nothing's the matter with me," I said, "I just process the colours differently." "How do you fix it?" they asked with good intentions. "You don't fix it. In fact, fixing it would suggest something's wrong," I replied. "You can't see the six. That's what's wrong," was the response.

After a short pause, and clearly having lost sight of the fact that I was talking to my children, I retorted defensively, "Anyway, you can't *not* see the six! I can see a perfectly good pattern that hasn't been ruined by this six you speak of."

So, at this point let me ask you this. Who's right? Is there a six or isn't there? When I ask an audience, there is usually a polite silence. Occasionally someone says generously, "you're both right." Of course, the vast majority can see the six and they side with my kids. Majority rules.

The fact is, we can never see this the same, no matter how much we want to see it from the other person's perspective. Although this metaphor relies on a physical difference in order to demonstrate that two people could both look at the same thing and yet see something completely different, the exact same thing is true of a belief. The way a belief filters and distorts our perception of reality.

Let's consider John. You know John, the nice guy. You've known John all your life. You trust John. He has your interests at heart. Always a kind word and friendly smile. Then one day you meet John and he's a bit "off" with you, he's not himself. What goes through your mind? What would you do? That's not like John, I wonder if he's OK? So you ask, "John, is everything OK?" We'd make an exception for John's behaviour because we'd filter it through our belief that John's a friend, a nice guy.

Unlike the other John. You know, John the bastard! Wouldn't trust John as far as you could throw him. Always talks behind people's backs. Bad-mouth everyone! What if John was particularly nice to you? What if, for no reason, he enthusiastically says, "Good Morning" with a beaming smile. What would you think? Exactly. "What does John want?!"

Your belief is the filter through which you see everything and this affects how you experience situations and how you react. Think back to the Win Learn Change model I shared in Chapter 8. Boris Becker may have lost the match, but he believed he learnt from it and became better. He believed it was a learning experience, which was far more important and relevant than the result in the long run because it allowed him to stay in a resourceful state.

How about some easier questions: Is there a God? Are ghosts real? Do extraterrestrials exist *out there?*

Naturally we'll all have views on the big three. Yes, no, don't know, don't want to know. Even though we may have a strong sense of certainty (belief) about our particular perspective, the one thing that we can probably agree on is there is only actually one true reality. We can't all be right. I mean, there may well be multiple realities but I just don't think we have time for that debate too! So for sake of expediency let's just say that in this life or the next someone ultimately will be proved right! However, being right and needing to be right are a world apart.

In fact I would go as far as to say that the question "who is right" is the problem. It's a redundant question if we're simply looking at how our beliefs provoke our emotions, and how our emotions impact our ability to achieve our goals and ambitions. A better question might be, are my guiding beliefs aligned with my desired outcomes? Am I seeing this situation in such a way that it triggers resourcefulness and drives consistent high performance? Put simply, is the way I am seeing this situation holding me back or propelling me forwards?

Going back to my eye-test metaphor, it's determined by what we want. If we were to agree that the desired outcome is to see a number six when we look at the image, then those that can see it are clearly processing it in an optimum way. However, if we agreed that our desire was to see a pattern not spoiled by the number six, then surely I and the other deutans out there are the ones processing it optimally.

Our beliefs are precisely that: they are ours. Beliefs are feelings of certainty that we have about a whole range of things. Whatever comes after the following are just our take on things:

Life is. . . .
People are. . . .
The world is. . . .

I am. . . .

Again, the desired outcome here is to find a strategy that enables us to frame things in a way that causes us to hang out in a positive mind more often with the sole purpose of being able to drop into flow on a more regular basis.

Performance hack: Pick a card

Lucy was reflecting on a presentation that she'd given the day before and I asked her what card would represent her level of performance. Where two is low and Ace is high. I asked her to picture in her mind what the group would have seen from the time she walked into the room until the time she left.

She'd been a bit distracted, she'd arrived late, hadn't really taken the time to gather herself and she seemed to rush through her words. So, when reflecting on her speech, what she'd said, her pace and tone of voice, and her body language, the way she stood and moved, along with her eye contact with the group, or lack of, she didn't feel she'd done a particularly good job. She gave herself a three, the three of diamonds.

We considered the question, what if, before walking into her next meeting or presentation, or for that matter any situation, she simply assumed the mindset that corresponds to a different playing card?

Think about it for a moment. What if you could choose the card in advance?

Before walking in, or just before hitting "join Zoom meeting," what if you paused and considered which card represents how you want to lean into the situation? How do you want to be? How do you want to come across to others? What would *being* a picture card look like?

This is so much more than just "trying to be positive." By preselecting the Jack, Queen, or King, our whole system shifts to meet that expectation. How we think, how we move, and how we behave.

Taking a moment to proactively choose how you want to lean in makes it our choice to be in a positive mind and, for sure, way easier to slip into flow and just be in the moment. Every morning, every meeting, every training session, you can pick the card. Just as well choose an Ace!

Chapter 12

CYCLE TO FLOW

This is probably a good time for a confession. In my enthusiasm to communicate to you the value of flow states, there is a chance that I might have made it sound all too easy to gain access to the zone. Aligning a selection of the external and internal triggers and shifting from negative mind to positive mind will, for sure, assist in the journey to that super-focused state of consciousness but, and it's a big but, there's a good reason why it's so elusive. That reason is the initial phase of what's known as the flow cycle.

The flow cycle: Struggle/Release/Flow/Recovery

In the summer of 2020, many people around the world were deep into their first experience of lockdown. It felt like the stress response was permanently in the fully on position. Lots of adrenaline and cortisol, and not many feel-good chemicals.

Feel-good chemicals like serotonin and oxytocin are involved in generating a sense of well-being. Unlike dopamine, which rewards forward motion and focuses our attention on things outside of our body, serotonin and oxytocin focus our attention inwards and cause us to feel good in our immediate sphere of existence. It feels good in the moment. Oxytocin is known as the love drug. It's released when we hug family and friends, sometimes even pictures of family that hold meaning for us can cause a release of oxytocin.

For all of the obvious reasons, they were in short supply at a time when they were most needed. Of course, we were all living through our own version of lockdown, but let's just look at things through the lens of our work life. For some it provided a welcome opportunity to spend more time at home; for others they were thrown into turmoil that involved setting up a home office, juggling work and home schooling, being made redundant, or having to look for a complete change in career. As someone who used to fly around the world speaking to large groups of people gathered indoors, it will be no surprise to you when I say that my business fell off a cliff. A hundred percent of my 12-month pipeline of work disappeared within a matter of days. It wasn't ideal; however, I soon rationalised that compared to many others I had nothing really to complain about. Also, I'd spent 25 years spouting the message that it's not what happens, it's how you respond that counts, so I was about to find out the true meaning of *walk your talk*.

Coincidentally, it was around that time that I started looking into this intriguing topic called flow. I figured that in demanding circumstances having access to flow would be a tremendous asset, which of course it would. However, this wasn't to improve my golf game or my harmonica playing, I needed it to rebuild my business at a time when I wasn't feeling very flowy. Even though I was gaining an understanding of things like the flow triggers and doing my best to frame the situation in ways that would help me get into my positive mind, I was still finding it almost impossible to get into the zone in a meaningful way. Putting together project plans, re-writing training programmes to suit virtual delivery platforms, trying to understand what these things called virtual delivery platforms were! This brings me to the focus of this chapter: How do you get into flow when life sucks and the work is hard, really hard?

Step 1 – Struggle phase

I've since spoken to many people who were in a similar position as me. They got the gist of flow but were struggling to find it. It's easy to beat ourselves up and feel like we're doing something wrong. One client I talked to said she couldn't find the motivation to start writing a book she'd been commissioned to write. The deadline was drawing near and the pressure was building, which didn't seem to be helping. She felt like she'd wasted the whole of lockdown, which should have been the perfect opportunity to get stuck in, and this made her feel even more guilty. She'd make a start but couldn't get fully immersed. Even though this was an important project, other priorities always found their way to the top of her to-do list.

But then, with a matter of months to go before the planned completion date, suddenly everything changed. She said it was like a switch got flicked and she went all-in. It was all she could think about. Now everything else felt like a distraction. All she wanted to do was to get back to the book.

She asked me, "Why couldn't I get myself into that position sooner? What was going on in my brain?" It was such a drastic state change, what happened neurochemically that set everything in motion? I suspect the impending deadline had something to do with providing that extra motivation, in so much that it provided the extra push needed to get her through this initial phase of the flow cycle. It was hard, but it had been hard for a year or more. The difference was this time she kept going until she broke through.

Flow is an interesting and highly desirable state but we need to appreciate that the early stages of hard work and focus are going to feel like agitation, stress, and confusion. That's the adrenaline system kicking in. In the same way that we wouldn't start a heavy workout at the gym or go for a long run without warming up a little, our brain also needs to warm up and start to figure out which circuits are going to be active. It's unreasonable to think we're just going to switch on our laptop and start banging out our best work, we need to accept that when we're doing challenging work, there's a period of agitation and stress that precedes dropping into these highly concentrated states.

Before we get into the groove we need the dopamine reward system to keep us on the right path. We talked earlier about rewarding ourselves, not just for hitting our milestones, but just for being in the act of taking action. These small boosts put us on the right path and are essential to get us through this struggle phase. You'll remember in Chapter 7 on persistence that it's the dopamine that smacks down the adrenaline and suppresses the quit reflex. Then, when we are on the right path and we hit a milestone, the dopamine tends to tighten our focus more for that activity. Now you're starting to wire in the behaviours that make people good at building momentum, and you start to see the agitation and stress as the gateway to get to the focus component. If you continue to reward the effort process, soon enough you start to feel joy. It's like, yes, I've got a lot of adrenaline in my system, but I'm on the right path; it feels good to walk up that hill, so to speak. This applies to writing a book, filling out a job application, or building a business.

The misunderstanding around how these circuits work has led to this idea that there's some secret entry point, maybe marked "flow" on the door, and there's an elevator that takes you up to that door. Sometimes that's just not how it works, and anyone who has done well in any career or athletic pursuit knows this. Unfortunately, there's almost an obsession with the idea that it's all supposed to feel good, and it does feel good, but there's a whole staircase we may have to climb that can feel lousy before we get to enter. Having an understanding of the four stages of the flow cycle is helpful because if you know where you are, you know what to expect. And you know where you're going next.

So, if we're going to struggle let's at least hack the struggle gracefully. Mindset matters for struggle. If you have a fixed mindset, and you don't think you can get better, or you're just going to stay stuck and struggle, there's no way through. You have to have a growth mindset to proceed through struggle because when we're in struggle, our brain is spiraling and going in hard loops. We literally don't have the cognitive capacity to remember what to do to get ourselves out of struggle. Therefore, it makes sense to make a list of what works for you and pin the list on the wall next to your desk or pop a Post-it® note on your monitor. My list usually includes: epic self-talk to reward myself for being on the path, 15 minutes of breathwork, EDM music, red wine.

Step 2 – Release phase

In the struggle phase, we can't keep our mind off the problem. In the release phase, we take our mind off the problem. We literally stop doing what we're doing. We relax. What works best for release is low-grade physical exercise. Long walks are phenomenal release activities. So are gardening, building model aeroplanes, anything that's slightly tactile and slightly physical.

We're playing with the deep embodiment trigger here for release. So, what are we doing in release? We are passing a problem through our conscious mind to our subconscious mind. That's what's going on. Flow takes place once the subconscious can take over. Nitric oxide flushes into our system; the stress hormones get flushed out of our system. The interesting thing about release is that, because we're going to be in struggle, we want to build release into our schedule.

For example, I work from 7 a.m. to 9 a.m. most mornings, and then I take my dog for a walk. It's a release walk. The good news is, if I was in flow during my work session, the walk actually functions like a recovery period. If I was in struggle, the walk functions as a release trigger. The key here is it needs to be a low-grade activity.

Flow is a high-energy state and it's what comes next in the cycle. We don't want to deplete our energy stores by doing a really hard workout. Any activity in the release phase needs to be nice 'n easy.

One of the things that is tricky about the release phase, especially for peak performers, is they don't want to stop working. So, the reframe here is that during the release phase, you're literally programming your subconscious to solve the problem for you. That's not just a positive spin; there's science to back up that claim. Not that you need any: we've all had the experience of working through a tough project or wrestling with a complex problem and then you take a break and sleep on it and the ideas show up the next day in the shower or during the drive into the office. We talk about *priming questions* in Chapter 11. They are a great way to set off the release phase or make a statement about your intentions.

When I was writing *Unashamedly Superhuman*, I'd often finish the day and take 10 minutes to prime my mind for the following day. I'd write something like, "Tomorrow when I'm writing the chapter on 'One, Two, Three Minds,' I want to connect the colour blind story, the milkshake data, link it to the workplace and somehow make it factual and funny. Just the bare facts. We don't have to stitch it together. I just want some of the specifics about the particular problem I'm trying to solve. Write them down, and then go about your business, get some exercise, eat dinner, watch TV, lights out."

We have a pattern recognition system in our brain, and if you give it a specific problem it will keep trying to solve it. It doesn't happen automatically and it doesn't always work, but it works enough of the time to make it worth our while.

Steps 3 and 4 — Flow phase and recovery phase

The last two phases of the flow cycle I like to call the fun stuff. Everyone loves being in the flow state, and recovering afterwards is also pleasant if done right. If we're struggling to get into a piece of work or get into a long training session for that matter, just knowing that we're headed to the promised land of flow as well as some scheduled recovery time afterwards gives us a good enough reason to crack on. Both trigger a little dopamine to grease the wheels.

We've already spent a good amount of time looking at flow and in the next section of the book, "Tapping into Physiology," we take a deep dive into active recovery. For now I just want to stress the importance of getting the balance right. Flow is an exceptionally productive state, but whenever we're running on adrenaline and dopamine, albeit combined with the feel-good chemicals, serotonin and endorphins, it is nonetheless a tremendous drain on our energy stores. At some point we run out and will need to replenish our stores before we go back in. Coming down after an hour or two in the zone is not unlike having a mild hangover. What goes up must come down. Sometimes you can have too much of a good thing, including flow.

We don't want to deplete all the dopamine because we want more flow tomorrow. If we do, we must reflect that in our recovery strategy.

The first thing to learn about recovery is to protect your schedule. You've got to make time for it. Recovery is a skill, and it requires persistence. The following are a couple of simple hacks that can help at the end of a big day. Reading 20–30 pages of a book that sits outside your core subject. Most people find fiction to be better than nonfiction. The de-compression effect will add a lot more cognitive flow to your life. Another good flow practice is to use the power of visualisation. On the back end of a flow experience, just take a few minutes to reflect on how good it felt when you were skiing down the mountain, banging out a tune on the piano, or just after you came off stage at your company conference. One of my triathlon coaches suggested, last thing at night just before checking out for the day, that I replay in my mind sections of a training session when I was in the groove. It not only feels good in the moment, it trains the brain to recognise the very thing you want more of.

I'd like to finish this session by shining a light on *play* as a way of practicing how to get into flow. Not work, just play. We talked about how many of us have dropped into flow accidentally and how we don't always know how we got there. The thing is, like any other skill, we need to practice it. One way of doing that is by remembering the times and the activities we used to participate in where it was easy to lose ourselves in that activity. How many people have stopped playing guitar, writing poetry, or painting with water colours – activities packed with flow triggers—just because these "hobbies" are typically activities that no longer tick the *important to do* box. Certainly not important enough to prioritise when we're busy being serious about serious things.

If you've been blocked from flow lately, take this as permission to play. At the time of writing this, we're deep into the winter months. Many people are heading off to the ski slopes for a fix of flow. Much of the early research into flow came from action-adventure sports, particularly extreme snow sports.

In his book *Stealing Fire*,[1] Steven Kotler talks about the origins of snowboarding. He says in the 1980s, snowboarding was a

[1] Kotler, S. and Wheal, J., (2018), *Stealing Fire: How Silicon Valley, the Navy SEALs and Maverick Scientists Are Revolutionizing the Way We Live and Work*, DeyStrBks, Reprint edition.

banned sport at most resorts. The original free riders got around this ban by taking their show into the backcountry, free from resort rules and free to interpret the terrain any way they wanted. This freedom translated into far greater opportunities for creativity, which triggered more flow, which further enhanced creativity.

All this flowy creativity supercharged the rate of innovation, jacking up performance, and when captured on video, looked like such ridiculous fun that everyone wanted in on the action—particularly a guy by the name of Shane McConkey. Among other things, McConkey is known for integrating the word *free* into extreme sports. Nowadays, the *free* prefix is used in all kinds of action sports. Free surfing, free skiing, and free riding, referring to mountain biking. This shift from "extreme" to "free" emphasised self-expression and de-emphasised winning, and especially de-emphasised the idea of a solitary winner.

As long as free-riders were seeing interesting lines and riding those lines in interesting ways, they were winning. No longer was the fastest person down the mountain the best athlete on the mountain. To really win, you had to be creative. Creativity became the way athletes judged success. Did it look stylish? Was it innovative? Did it add anything to the conversation? These days, imagination and innovation form the basis for how these athletes are judged and judge themselves.

Whether focusing on being up a snow-capped mountain or back at the office snowed under with an endless list of things to do, dropping into a flow state has proven over and over to play its part in adding to both our experience and the end result. We've all heard the phrase, "Winning isn't everything; it's the taking part that counts." Well, when it comes to flow, taking part is everything; you just happen to win as well. What can you do this week that would make it easy for you to experience a flow state?

Chapter 13

UNDER
THE RADAR

I was hosting a meeting for my team of 12 sales reps. It was a low-key affair with only two agenda items: look over the results from the previous quarter and say goodbye to the team. I called the meeting for a Saturday because Wales was playing England in a rugby international at the Arms Park stadium that afternoon. After an enjoyable, eight-year career in sales, the plan was for the team to attend this short review meeting, and then as a thank you from me, we'd attend the big game, followed by the appropriate celebrations that always follow a Welsh win over the Englanders.

Unbeknownst to the 12 of us, the president of the organisation was about to enter the room. This was someone who, in the eight years that I'd spent at this company, I'd only ever seen in corporate literature. Nobody in the room had ever laid eyes on him. It was incongruous for him to appear at this gathering of lowly sales reps. My boss, my sales manager, was there, but it made no sense for my boss's boss to be there. Let alone his boss's, boss's, boss's, boss's, boss's, boss's boss! His attendance was a shock to say the least.

That shock was nothing compared to what was to come. To protect the innocent, let's call the main man, Chuck. The meeting was due to run from 9.30 a.m. to 12.30 p.m. We were an hour in when *it* happened. Chuck entered. His energy alone could fill a room. He was also a big guy. A six-footer and barrel chested. Suited and booted.

My boss, who at the time was addressing the group, upon recognising Chuck, picked his jaw up off the floor and asked, with understandable hesitation, "Uh, hi, it's Chuck, isn't it?" "That's right," our surprise guest boomed. "Thought I'd drop by and say howdy to the team." Did I mention Chuck was American? Oh yes, he was very American. Confident and compelling. "Who does this on a Saturday?" he asked rhetorically.

"Mind if I say a few words to the team?" He explained that he didn't get to the United Kingdom often, that he was a guest of a dignitary who was hosting him at the afternoon's big match. Somehow he'd heard about our Saturday meeting and thought he'd surprise us. Then it happened. "Last year was challenging for everyone in our industry," he started, "But I have to say, the results here in Wales were nothing short of outstanding." So far, so good. We were all transfixed; after all, it was Chuck.

"The next six months is going to be equally challenging. A lot of change ahead, but we have a strategy that will see us through these choppy waters," he reassured us. All eyes were on Chuck; we were like first-year students, when the headmaster was talking.

"However," Chuck exclaimed, left arm abruptly raised, fist clenched, "That's not what I came here to say. I traveled here, to Cardiff, an hour earlier than I needed to, to tell you just one thing. . . ." His voice lowered to a purposeful whisper, "I believe in you," he said earnestly. He paused for a few seconds, while it sank in. Then repeated it in case we'd somehow missed it, "I believe in you." He paused again, each person present received a good two-second eye contact (it seemed longer). "But the question is. . . ." We leaned in, you could hear a pin drop, that is until, at the top of his New York voice, he boomed, "DO" pause "YOU" pause "BELIEVE?" whilst pointing directly at me. The room gulped with me. Eyes widened. Slightly scared, heavily startled. What? we all thought.

Again, this time to Mike, who sat at the back, "COME ON," Chuck bellowed, "DO. YOU. BELIEVE?" My god, the penny dropped, he wants us to join in. "Yeeesss," we replied awkwardly. None in unison, none of us with any conviction. "NO, COME ON, ON YOUR FEET. DO. YOU. BELIEVE?" You could practically hear the collective thought of the group. "Does he know we're British? We don't do this here. We can't. Genetically!"

Undaunted, like a true leader, he drove on, "DO. YOU. BELIEVE?" The room shifted slightly, "YES" we half shouted, this time all together. "DO. YOU. BELIEVE?" "YES" The volume doubled. "DO YOU BELIEVE?" "YEEEES," we punched back. "DO YOU BELIEVE?" "YEEEEEES!" We cheered, arms aloft, matching Chuck's energy, volume for volume.

"DO YOU BELIEVE?" "YEEEEEEEEEES WE BELIEVE."

The room at a fever pitch, his work done, Chuck triumphantly strode out of the room. He just walked out. He didn't return. Time stood still. Awoken to what had just happened, caught in a state of over-motivation, we suddenly landed back in the room. My boss turned to us, his tone pitched somewhere between doubt and hope, and asked, nervously, "Do you believe?" We looked at him, looked at each other, back to him, and in unison said, "No, not really." The meeting ended. How could it continue after that?

I left the company the following week, but this arresting experience lived with me, haunted me. Of all the things he could have said, all the other pearls of wisdom that he could have shared with us, he chose to do that. I don't know why he felt the need to challenge us in that way, but it seemed really, really important to him, and he was the boss. The big boss. I thought about that day often. It took a year or so before it dawned on me that really all he was trying to do was to motivate us. His method was a little niche but his intentions were pure. The definition of *motivation* is something that initiates, guides, and maintains goal-oriented behaviours. It's the invisible ingredient that energises us and gets us to do something.

It may not have had the desired effect in that hotel in Cardiff, but his 10-minute speech provoked me to go in search of what it is that inspires people to reach for more and was the beginning of what's turned out to be a 25-year career as a professional speaker, occasionally even a motivational one at that! Maybe the man was a genius after all.

Under the radar refers to those things that go unnoticed. Unlike the big booming voice of Chuck, these are the more subtle things that go a long way in activating your *superhuman*, and being unashamed to do so, not visible to the outside world. The classic analogy often used to explain success in life is the iceberg model. Above the water line we can see the results people achieve; we can also see the actions and behaviours that enabled them to hit their sales, build their business, or get their body beach ready for the summer. We can see how they did it but we can't see how they got themselves to do it. What motivated them.

Outside in or inside out

Motivation is the force that compels us to take action. So, what is it that truly motivates you? Think about your motivation for reading this book. Are you trying to pick up some tips and tricks to help you to go to the next level in your career or maybe you're looking to find some science-backed strategies to help you help others or motivate your team perhaps? If so, that's extrinsic motivation because achieving better results is external reinforcement. If, on the other hand, you are more interested in learning about human behaviour and understanding the systems that drive you, then you are intrinsically motivated as you are the driving force of your motivation. In all likelihood both have a part to play in the pursuit of our biggest personal and professional goals.

Of course, we want to be rewarded for our efforts, financial being perhaps the most obvious. As one of my astute clients once put it, there's no mission without margin. The carrot and the stick are the extrinsic factors that get us up early and keep us out late, whether by necessity or design, but what is the X factor that can add the fire in our belly, the spring in our step and the *joie de vivre* that make the journey as exhilarating and rewarding as reaching our destination?

Motivation from the inside out

Despite a relentless self-improvement market peppering us with endless tips and tricks on how to live better, healthier, wealthier lives, the reality is the vast majority of people need something more than the promise of fast cars, fine dining, and riches beyond their wildest dreams. There's more to it than just BELIEVE and succeed.

Even if we know something is bad for us that doesn't always induce a change in our behaviour. Those of us who smoke (or have smoked) know we're increasing our chances of any number of illnesses each time we light up. Do we still take a drag? Of course we do! It's not easy turning common sense into common practice. Enter the power of flow states. Specifically, that sense of effortlessness that can propel us past the limits of normal motivation. We're only just beginning to understand where this added drive comes from. When the psychologist Mihaly Csikszentmihalyi did his initial research into flow, people frequently called the state "addictive" and admitted to going to exceptional lengths to get another fix. And it's understandable. Negative feelings quickly get replaced by empowering alternatives. Enjoyment replaces boredom, helplessness turns into a feeling of control, detachment gives way to feeling engrossed in an activity. In other words, when we're rewarded from the inside out, all's well in the world.

One of the organisations that I regularly work with is the professional services company Deloitte. I've benefited greatly from working with its teams all over the world. Their commitment to their clients and to each other has been a source of inspiration to me. At the company's *Centre for the Edge*, co-founder John Hagel made a global study of the world's most innovative, high-performing business teams, and he found that the teams and organisations that went the furthest were always the ones tapping into passion and finding flow. He said they all have one thing in common when it comes to goal setting. . . .

It seems their lives are purposefully built around what we'll call mission-critical goals. It's the challenging nature of these goals that is the first secret to success. It turns out that if you want the largest increase in motivation and productivity, then challenging goals lead to the best outcomes. But how challenging exactly? We touched on this earlier in the book when we looked at the flow trigger, skills/challenge balance. According to the flow theory, flow experience occurs when skills are neither overmatched nor underutilised to meet a given challenge. The balance of challenge and skill is delicate. The goal should be significant. It should be inspirational and aggressive yet realistic. How inspirational? Well, not so much that you can't sleep at night but enough that you can't wait to get up in the morning. So, what does inspirational and exciting mean and how can we make it happen?

Does the probability of achieving a goal go up or down if the goal is easy, moderate, or impossible? When people set goals, whether nutritional, fitness, learning, relationship, or business-related, if it's too *in reach* it doesn't recruit enough of the autonomic nervous system to make pursuit likely. In other words, if it's too easy, people lose interest. If it's too lofty and too intangible, the dopamine doesn't kick in either. It turns out that the likelihood of being engaged doubles if our goals are realistic but truly challenging.

Psychologists believe mission-critical goals impact two things: persistence and focus, two more important factors in determining performance. However, for these mission-critical goals to really work their magic, there is one other key factor that needs to be in place and that's total commitment. The point here is that when we choose a goal, even if it means willfully accepting a target given to us by our manager or a change in direction provoked by unforeseen global circumstances, we commit to that goal.

I may have mentioned once or twice that to provoke me to get a clearer understanding of this goal-setting principle I took on the IRONMAN® triathlon challenge, my BHAG. At the time of setting the goal I may have had no idea how I was going to achieve it but it was willfully set.

When we frame our thinking in such a way that we willfully decide what our desired outcome is, a sense of purpose kicks up a gear, driving more attention and more focus on achieving the result and therefore more flow. It's like taking that January enthusiasm and sprinkling it over your objectives. So, what are your mission-critical goals? Just one or two objectives that are going to fire you up from the inside out over the next six to 12 months. I say one or two because it's key to avoid goal distraction. One or two major goals a year is optimum.

Mastering your own motivation

So, let's turn our attention to the adventures that lie ahead and start by focusing on perhaps the single most important factor that will determine whether you'll turn your vision into results. Let's talk about passion.

In the past I've attended many personal development seminars that, although incredibly motivational and for me at the time tremendously valuable, never quite hit the mark. I never felt particularly comfortable when the guru would shout LIVE WITH PASSION!

Passion has been declared everything from the secret to success in business to the foundation of a meaningful life. I just wasn't comfortable with that particular word. It may well be the magic pill, but what if you don't know what you're passionate about? I found it difficult to connect the word *passion* to things like getting up and going to work or trying to motivate myself to get to the gym. However, I've since managed to develop a much more pragmatic understanding of not just why it's so important, but also how to go about framing things in such a way that we can get the benefits of this all-encompassing emotion.

OK, let me start by demystifying the word. For starters, from a tactical perspective, why is passion important? Well, to put it simply, it's a profound focusing mechanism. We pay more attention to those things we believe in. That makes sense. And we know the golden rule: flow follows focus. Focused attention creates the ultimate gateway drug to high performance and productivity. It drives us and directs our efforts.

Moreover, since flow is among the most motivating states on earth, any experience that consistently generates that state is an experience we will go out of our way to get more of. It's why surfers will get up at four in the morning and drive for three hours to catch a wave. Or why video gamers will play games for 10 hours straight. In other words, the pursuit of flow produces extreme levels of internal motivation.

Being in the zone is the payoff. This flips the conventional way of thinking about motivation entirely on its head. It's no longer a matter of doing X to get Y, but rather doing X for X's sake. Just like our free sports enthusiasts, it's not all about winning or losing, it's just about searching for that next high. In a nutshell, passion leads to focus, which generates self-motivation.

So, how do we discover our passion and amp up our focus? Well, that's where our adventure comes in. When we considered the question: What words do you associate with going on an adventure? the answers weren't necessarily positive. Exciting, fulfilling, exhilarating but also challenging, risky, and let's say character-building. However, as we discussed previously, despite that, the word *adventures* does compel us to move towards them. We seem to attach value to them. And anything we value, anything that is important to us, creates a dotted line to passion.

If that sounds a bit too much like personal development speak, let's look at the science. We've talked about the motivational effect that dopamine has, and for cultivating passion, this is a big deal. First, dopamine is a focusing chemical. It helps us pay more attention to the task at hand. This enhances learning and drives progress, and both are key to cultivating passion. Second, dopamine tunes into what is called "signal to noise ratios" in the brain, which is a fancy way of saying it affects how we see challenging situations, and it helps us to find solutions, seeing patterns. That's creativity. That is why creative ideas tend to spiral. One good idea leads to the next and the next. Right?

Last, dopamine is a feel-good drug. It's one of the brain's principal reward chemicals and, as I've mentioned before, it's extremely addictive. This addiction is key to passion. The more dopamine you get, the more addictive the experience, and the more addictive the experience, the more you can't wait to do it again.

Take that feeling into the adventure of moving ahead in your organisation or pushing through your annual targets or running a 10K for charity or whatever else it is that you've got your eye on for the year ahead. One thing's for sure, it's only going to help. It will help us to be one of the few who don't just set New Year's resolutions, but who actually go ahead and do what they have to do in order to achieve them.

Crystal clear – Goal stacking

"If one does not know to which port one is sailing, no wind is favourable." — Seneca

I'm saying that as though I know who Seneca was. I just received a book from a friend. It's called *The Daily Stoic.* I love what it says on the inside cover, which reads: "Long the secret weapon of history's great figures, from emperors to artists and activists to fighter pilots, the principles of stoicism have shone brightly through the centuries as a philosophy for doers." I love that, "a philosophy for doers." It goes on to say, "Tested in the lab of human experience, over the last two thousand years, this timeless knowledge is essential to navigating the complexities of modern life."

Anyway, turns out Seneca was one of the Roman stoics. "If one does not know to which port one is sailing, no wind is favourable."

So, let's talk about clarity. More specifically, how to deal with a lack of clarity. The *V* and the *U* of the VUCA world we previously mentioned refers to *volatility* and *uncertainty*. The antidotes to which are Vision and Clarity, respectively. Uncertainty has a nasty habit of creeping in and infecting different areas of life. I don't know about you, but sometimes it feels difficult to know exactly where to focus my attention or even which task to do first.

The point being, right now, it can be somewhat challenging to stay laser focused on the direction of our lives. Being clear on where we want to go is incredibly important for flow, and incredibly difficult to tie down when so much is up in the air in the wider world. Without clear goals, obviously it's difficult to direct our attention. The prefrontal cortex gets stuck in analysis mode. The part of our brain that drives complex behaviours like decision-making becomes overactive.

The good news is we don't need to map out our entire destiny in detail in order to harness the benefits of clarity. We just need to pick a direction and move. As Phil Jones, UK Managing Director of Brother, put it, "Our DOT, our direction of travel." We can then stack our goals underneath. Underneath our DOT are our six- to 12-month mission-critical goals, and beneath them are our daily focus goals. Let's take a closer look at each level.

Goal stacking: What, why, and how?

Level 1: Direction of travel

The purpose of this top level is to generate just that, purpose. It's less a destination and more the reason we do the things we do. It's aspirational, meaningful, and worthwhile. This drives norepinephrine and dopamine into our system.

When working with corporate clients who are endeavouring to clarify their respective company's purpose, I would always point them in the direction of Patrick Lencioni's work, particularly his book *The Advantage*.[1] In it he asks the question: How does an organisation go about figuring out why it exists? He goes on to say that it starts by asking the question: How do we contribute to a better world? Sceptics who think this sounds soft or ethereal need to remember that this is not the end of the clarification process and that it is critical to create a framework for more tactical decisions. He says that usually the first answer that leaders come up with is not ideal enough, for example, "We help companies use technology to do more business with their partners" or "We pave driveways so people can get in and out of their houses."

Those are a start, but they're certainly not lofty enough. The next question that needs to be asked, and asked again and again until it leads to the highest purpose or reasons for existence, is: Why? Why do we do what we do? Why do we help companies use technology to do more business with their partners? Why do we pave driveways? Eventually, by answering that question again and again, a leadership team will get to a point where it's identified the most idealistic reason for their business. That point will be somewhere just shy of "to make the world a better place."

For example, the Apple Corporation's is: Make the best products on earth and to leave the world better than we found it.

Amazon's is: Our vision is to be earth's most customer centric company; to build a place where people can come to find and discover anything they might want to buy online.

Nike's is: Do everything possible to expand human potential.

These statements reflect the company's direction of travel, its North Star.

So how can we tap into purpose? How can we carve out our current direction of travel? A practical exercise that can shine a little light on your current vocational purpose would be helped by a process I run with teams to help them to dovetail their own

[1] Lencioni, P.M., (2012), *The Advantage: Why Organizational Health Trumps Everything Else in Business (J-B Lencioni Series)*, Jossey-Bass, 1st edition.

purpose with their respective organisation. Easier to do if you own your own business, but perhaps more challenging if you've recently joined a global corporation and you're not particularly familiar with its mission statement. It's a great exercise that helps to drill into both the logical and emotional reasons you go into the office every day. It's called the business card exercise.

I believe this is where the idea comes from the following.

In 1962, President John F. Kennedy visited National Aeronautics and Space Administration (NASA) for the first time. During his tour of the facility, he met a janitor who was carrying a broom down the hallway. The President then casually asked the janitor what he did for NASA, and the janitor replied, "I'm helping put a man on the moon."

Take a moment and reflect on this idea. The janitor knew something that most of us struggle with, the purpose of his work. He kept the building clean so that the scientists, engineers, and astronauts could focus on their mission of putting "man on the moon." They did not have to worry about spending their time on trash cans, bathrooms, or hallways. He did that for them. He saw where his contribution fit in the organisation. He connected his purpose with theirs. Level 1 of goal stacking is the part that most people forget about or simply don't know about.

So, imagine on the back of your business card it stated what you personally do for your business. Question one is simply: What do you do? Write down the phrase that describes your role. For me right now it might read: "Writes books and speaks at conferences." Factually accurate but hardly inspiring. No flow to speak of. OK, so next question. What does what you do enable others to do? This takes a little more thought. For me that may be: "Helps people get a better understanding of how to combine high performance and well-being." Better, but still biased towards logic more than emotion. Let's go again. What does that enable others to do? Of course, I don't have hard data for the next answer, so I have to go with my instincts or perhaps my best intentions: "Enables them to tap into their potential, mindset, and physiology."

So, what does that enable people to do? "Helps them to become better, smarter, and stronger." We're getting there.

What does that enable people to do? "Harness their inner power and achieve their greatest professional and personal goals." Boom!

Level 2: Mission-critical goals

The next level down we have our mission-critical goals. These goals are long-term, but not infinite. They'll be specific and measurable. Thinking big but believable big. Take on a promotion, exceed an annual target, or maybe learn a foreign language. If our DOT connects to our *why*, our mission-critical goals determine specifically *what* we're excited about achieving.

You don't need more than two or three of these chunky goals each year. My 12-month goals at the time of writing are to do a triathlon and write a book. That's great, but just knowing that doesn't mean they're going to happen. To make your mission-critical goals a reality, you have to break them down into manageable, daily focus goals.

Level 3: Daily focus goals

Finally, our daily focus goals are there to point out exactly what needs to be done. Daily activities that are the stepping stones to the achievement of our mission-critical goals that feed into our DOT, our North Star.

For my two goals, a daily focus goal might be to write a chapter. Or I know I need to put in 15 hours on the bike and in the pool this week, so I break that down into daily chunks to make sure it happens.

This is a goal stack and it generates a flow stack. Purpose, passion, and progress!

When it comes to getting into flow, this type of daily goal setting is crucial. You can never be too clear with your daily focus goals. The clearer you are about these tasks, the less you need to engage in "busy thinking" and the more easily you'll be able to release flow.

So, let me end this chapter with a question. DO YOU BELIEVE? :-)

Chapter 14

STAY IN THE NOW

What price for your attention?

An article in *the Guardian*[1] stated how senior Google, Twitter, and Facebook programmers, those who helped make their technology so addictive, are disconnecting themselves from the very social media platforms that they themselves created.

In the article, Justin Rosenstein talks about how he had tweaked his laptop's operating system to ban himself from Snapchat, which he compares to heroin, and imposed limits on his use of Facebook. He was particularly aware of the allure of Facebook "likes," which he describes as *"bright dings of pseudo-pleasure."* And Rosenstein should know; he was the Facebook engineer who created the "like" button in the first place, staying up all night coding a prototype of what was then called the "awesome" button.

The idea was soon copied by Twitter, Instagram, and countless other apps and websites. Research shows people touch, swipe, or tap their phone 2,617 times a day. Just to be clear, I'm not anti-phone nor anti-social media. Aside from relying on and enjoying both, I wouldn't even know where to begin to try to compete with the machines that appear to be running a large part of our lives. I am, however, anti-distraction. So, anything we can do to train our brain to be able to resist the beeps, dings, and urges to check our inbox whilst attempting to get important stuff done has a place in this book.

Let me start by raising the value of one of the few things right now that is within our control, our attention! It's a valued commodity and it would seem everyone wants a piece of it! We value money and we wouldn't throw that away, yet we are probably all guilty of throwing away our attention. Distractions fracture our attention, dissipating the focus needed to stay in the zone. We need to get seriously protective of our attention!

---

[1] Lewis, P., (2017), "'Our Minds Can Be Hijacked'": The Tech Insiders Who Fear a Smartphone Dystopia," *The Guardian*, 6 October. Available at: https://www.theguardian.com/technology/2017/oct/05/smartphone-addiction-silicon-valley-dystopia?CMP=share_btn_tw.

Eliminate distraction, amp up focus, and unlock flow.

It's happened to us all. Just when you're ready to knuckle down and get stuck into the most important item on your to-do list, the phone buzzes and the text, which will only take a moment to check, results in you having to search out an old email that you forward to a client who immediately calls you because your email reminded them about something they meant to ask you, which results in a chain of events that takes out your morning. Then your phone rings, and you're off again.

So, how do we guard against the distraction frenzy that is the 21st century? Dr Adam Gazzaley, a neuroscience professor at the University of San Francisco, has done a significant amount of foundational research on the subject.[2] First, he states that ignoring needs to be an active process. His work shows that there are two fundamental elements to focus: attending and ignoring. We're well versed at attending. That's us trying to stay focused. The ignoring piece is where the opportunity lies. In the same way that noise-cancelling headphones have their batteries drained simply by cancelling out noise in the environment, our mind spends a significant amount of energy trying to ignore what's going on around us too. Even if you feel like you can focus just fine, distractions in our environment are sapping our ability to pay attention.

He talks also about developing the ability to suppress spontaneity. For all of the tremendous value we gain from our phones, tablets, and computers, when it comes to getting and staying in the zone and doing the deep work, sometimes we need to kill the noise! Focus is the ability to resist the urge to indulge in spontaneous behaviour. Checking a text message, flicking through Instagram, snacking when we're not even hungry are all spontaneous actions that don't contribute to our predetermined goals. When you resist all these impulses the end-product, what you're left with, is focus. Pure and simple. Of course, spontaneity can be a great asset. Creativity is spontaneity. The key here is to let our creative spontaneity emerge once we're already in flow.

---

[2] Gazzaley, A., and Rosen, L.D., (2016), *The Distracted Mind: Ancient Brains in a High-Tech World*, MIT Press, Illustrated edition.

Performance hack: Planned focus sprints

Irrespective of the situations we find ourselves in, whether connected to sports, creative activities like producing art or writing music, or knuckling down to complete our to-do lists at work, one of the most rewarding things is to do so whilst experiencing a sense of flow. Here's a simple performance hack that pulls together some of the things we've discussed and taps into the golden rule: flow follows focus.

The Isolator
By HUGO GERNSBACK
MEMBER AMERICAN PHYSICAL SOCIETY

The author at work in his private study aided by the Isolator. Outside noises being eliminated, the worker can concentrate with ease upon the subject at hand.

Figure 14.1 The isolator

Figure 14.1 is no joke. This helmet was known as the isolator and was invented in 1925 by Hugo Gernsback. It was designed to help improve writing productivity by blocking out noise and limiting vision to anything other than what's in front of you. The perfect accessory for working at home. You may have trouble getting your hands on one, so let me offer you a less fetching but more portable option for tuning into the job at hand.

Some say that a great day begins the evening before. Taking a pen, paper, and 20 minutes or so, plan out the key areas of focus for the following day. This helps to prime the mind and tap into the seeking system we talked about earlier in the book. Answer questions like:

- What is the most important item in my schedule tomorrow?
- Why is that my priority?
- What specifically is my goal and what will success look like when I have achieved it?
- For a little extra drive, you could add a couple of lines about what will I gain by achieving my goal or what will it cost me if I don't?

Writing down these answers helps in a number of ways. Focus and clear your mind. The issue here is that while information, tasks, distractions, and responsibilities keep increasing, the space in our brains and the number of hours we have in our days remain the same. Writing down things is a simple yet powerful way to record anything and everything that has your attention. Once you write everything down, you'll notice a sense of relief, as if a weight was lifted off your shoulders. Even if you haven't *done* anything on your list just yet, there is a short period of transformation in which your brain goes from chaos to the first stages of order. Use this moment to take a deep breath and assure yourself that *you* are in control, that you're on your way to prioritisation and then action. Clarify your intentions. By having your goals, priorities, and intentions in front of you in writing, you're forced to literally see and evaluate them. You may even wake up in the morning with a head start as your unconscious mind has been putting in a shift whilst you've been sleeping blissfully.

With the prework done, we're enroute to designing our day in order to have as much focus time as possible. During this time, I mute all of my notifications, quit any distracting applications, pop on my noise-cancelling headphones, and turn on some music, preferably without lyrics. My personal favourite is a Spotify's playlist called Flow Triggers (other music platforms are available).

Why are they called focus sprints? We all understand what sprinting is: Short but intense bursts of energy that are meant to bring out the full extent of your body's capability. Focus sprints make use of those same intense energy bursts to help you overcome procrastination, channel your concentration, and get shit done.

You've probably heard of the circadian rhythm, the ebb and flow of energy over a 24-hour period. Well, the ultradian rhythm is similar just over a *shorter period of time*. This biological phenomenon helps explain why certain periods of the day are more productive than others. Typically, the human brain works best by focusing on a task in 90-minute intervals followed by 20-minute periods of rest. Pushing past this 90-minute mark can result in decreased focus. That's why focus sprinting is so effective. It takes advantage of your brain's natural rhythms to capitalise on the times you are at your peak performance.

The two keys to focus sprints are maintaining your focus and managing your rhythm. Before you start a series of sprints, set specific goals for each chunk of time. Whether you want to break one project up into smaller chunks or you want to tackle a different project for every sprint, establish expectations ahead of time and write them down.

Now that you have your goals laid out, set your timer. You don't necessarily need each sprint to be 90 minutes; it all depends on your personal rhythm. If you work better in 30-minute intervals with 5-minute breaks, go for it! The important thing is that you start paying attention to your natural productivity cycles and adapt to them. During the sprinting period, you must turn off all outside distractions and focus on a single task, no social media, no multitasking, no snack runs. Just 100 percent pure focus on the task at hand. If you find yourself consistently wanting to keep working past the timer, consider upping your sprint times. Know your limits, find your rhythm, and get to work. Tune in and keep your eye on the prize.

Obviously, some things on our to-do list, like taking care of emails, gathering information, or preparing for a meeting, don't require full immersion in the zone, whilst other tasks without a doubt require our undivided attention. For these, single-tasking beats multitasking hands down! If you're juggling a career, a family, home schooling, and an active social media friends group, it's easier said than done. However, if high performance and well-being are a priority, and in this book they are, this strategy is quite simply a game-changer.

Prepare to enjoy the fruitful return on your investment in your own attention. O*n your marks, get set, go!*

The secret sauce

Until relatively recently I would have struggled to look you in the eye with any conviction if I were pitching this next topic as worthy of discussion. In fact, when I started writing *Unashamedly Superhuman* this wasn't even on the list of potential topics. However, just months later I can't believe a book focusing on tapping into mindset wouldn't have this as its first pick in the draft of strategies for how to combine high performance and well-being.

I mentioned at the beginning of the book that I took a tremendous amount from Scott Carney's book, *What Doesn't Kill Us*, and that it was the hook on the front cover that drew me in: *How Freezing Water, Extreme Altitude, and Environmental Conditioning Will Renew Our Lost Evolutionary Strength.* This is because it opened up a whole new world of strategies to help me with my BHAG. This next topic was equally momentous for me. In some ways more so. Not only does it practically guarantee an uplift in performance and a greater sense of well-being, it has the added benefit of requiring no particular skill, zero financial investment, and this can all be achieved from the comfort of your own sofa. I'm talking about mindfulness and meditation. Now, I know some of you Type As are rolling your eyes, but bear with me, you're going to love the data on this!

In spite of my new-found enthusiasm, I still feel a little uncomfortable saying it aloud, *mindfulness and meditation.* I'm sure many of you have used such practices for years and swear by the many ways they have helped you to put a gap between stimulus and response, but personally, until recently, I've never really had the time. Or at least I've never made the time. I figured that I'd managed just fine for more than 50 years without actively attempting to spend my time in the *here and now.* I subscribed to the philosophies of, if you snooze you lose, and he or she who hesitates is lost. Surely there is a better use of our time when we're trying to forge ahead? That's what I thought. Now I don't know how I lived without them. The turning point came when I read some incontrovertible data that convinced me that such practices are not only the foundation of well-being but also a fast-track to high performance. They literally train our brain to blast through distraction, the kryptonite of flow.

So, after trying really hard not to, I decided to take a closer look at how to practice not being distracted. It turns out that just 15 minutes a day is enough to condition our mind's ability to stay focused. The scientific data backs up that claim.

Magnetic resonance imaging (MRI) scans have shown that something called gyrification occurs, which trains the brain to process information faster. Meditation has been shown to improve focus by causing an increase in the thickness of regions of the brain responsible for focused attention. Research done in the 1990s on Tibetan Buddhists found that long-term meditation produces brain waves in the gamma range.[3] These unusual brain waves arise primarily during what's called binding, the moment novel ideas snap together for the first time, otherwise known as a-ha moments. What this suggests is that meditation amplifies creativity. The problem is those monks had put in over 30,000 hours of cross-legged cushion time, not particularly practical for you and I. However, researchers then began to consider the impact of short-term meditation on mental performance. It showed that just 10–20 minutes a day relaxing into any activity that holds 100 percent of our attention and generates a calm, alert state of mind has an accumulative effect on developing our ability to focus our attention. Bearing in mind that we're quite literally doing nothing, it surely must be worth the effort, or lack of! If it still seems a bit *new age* for the busy Type A's, check this out. . . .

---

[3] Lutz, A., Greischar, L.L., Rawlings, N.B., Ricard, M., and Davidson, R.J., (2004), "Long-Term Meditators Self-Induce High-Amplitude Gamma Synchrony during Mental Practice," *Proceedings of the National Academy of Sciences*, 101(46): 16369–16373. https://doi.org/10.1073/pnas.0407401101.

Meditation has been seen to strengthen key brain networks for better focus, working memory, and mood. For instance, researchers noticed increased grey matter density in the hippocampus, a structure associated with storing memories and emotional control, and they found a decrease in grey matter in the amygdala, a structure associated with stress, fear, and anxiety, including our fight-or-flight response. This 15-minute-a-day habit, increases both composure and resilience.

It's been said that mindfulness, like sleep, diet, exercise, hydration, gratitude, and social integration improves everything. In my experience mindfulness leads to three Os:

Observation – Learning to notice when distracting thoughts pull away your focus.

Objectivity – Following the direction of your thoughts without judging and noticing how you feel and learning from it.

Openness – Accepting your emotions and recognising them as useful signals.

There are an infinite number of resources out there for those wishing to dive a little deeper. Recognising that I'm an enthusiast and a practitioner and by no means an expert, here are my ways of increasing mindfulness:

- Extreme uni-tasking
- Nature – down-regulates and soothes the nervous system
- Live mindfully – daily tasks like eating and listening to music
- Journaling
- Breathing exercises
- And, of course, meditation

Here are my two pennies' worth on how I've learned to incorporate that into a 20-minute daily practice. In a nutshell it seems to follow the ensuing pattern:

Focus attention on the breath
Attention wanders from the breath
Acknowledge current focus of attention
Redirect focus of attention to the breath.

OK try this. . . . , here goes. . . .

-Sit comfortably with an upright posture.

-Close your eyes, take a few initial deep breaths, in through the nose and long and steady out of the mouth. Feel the points of contact between you and the chair or floor. Focus on the sensations of sitting.

-Gradually become aware of the process of breathing. Pay attention to where you feel the breath most clearly. Either in the nostrils or in the rising and falling of the abdomen. Don't try and breathe in a particular way, just notice it.

-Every time your mind wanders in thought, gently bring it back to the sensation of breathing.

-As you focus on your breath you may notice that other perceptions and sensations continue to appear– sounds, feelings in the body, and emotions. Simply notice them in your field of awareness and then return to the sensation of your breathing.

-The moment you realise that you have been lost in thought, notice the present thought itself as an object to focus on. Then return your focus to your breath.

-Continue in this way as you witness how sights, sounds, emotions, sensations, and even thoughts rise and pass away.

If, like me, you really need the science to get you over the line on this one, here goes. There is solid data that meditation improves mood, cognition, brain function, gyrification, stress reduction, and focus. Here's how.

Mood – Meditation increases dopamine and serotonin levels by stimulating regions of the brain that are associated with positivity and happiness.

Cognition – Meditation improves cognitive function, mindfulness, and the ability to sustain focus by increasing grey matter, brain volume, and cerebral blood flow.

Brain function – Meditation increases whole brain function by synchronising the left and right hemispheres of the brain, while increasing balance and amplitude in alpha, theta, and delta brain wave patterns.

Gyrification – MRI scans have shown that meditation increases cortical folding, which allows the brain to process information faster. The effects of gyrification are highly implicated as being positively related to intelligence.

Stress reduction – Meditation decreases stress and anxiety by down regulating cortisol and adrenaline creating a state of deep relaxation in which our breathing, pulse rate, blood pressure, and metabolism are lowered.

Focus – Meditation improves focus by causing an increase in cortical thickness in regions of the brain responsible for attention.

Difficult to argue with all of that. Mic dropped. NAMASTE :-)

Doing positive

So, let's go back to the beginning of this part and re-run the conversation that I had with my boss.

After a long, soul-destroying week of failure and rejection my sales manager would often try to motivate me with a rousing pep talk. "Be positive, Jim," was well intentioned but ineffectual. What I needed to hear was, "Do this, then this, followed by this. . . . Do these specific things and you will feel so focused and positive that you are going to want to make that extra sales call."

Tapping into our mindset has put a spotlight on a range of those *things*. A process that we can depend on to ensure that we're in the optimum state of mind, giving us access to all of our skills and abilities, and the best possible chance of feeling and performing at our best.

Strategies, not straplines. We're SMARTER than that now.

Part IV

STRONGER – TAPPING INTO PHYSIOLOGY

As you have no doubt realised by this point, we are all capable of far more than we realise. So far we've covered tapping into potential and mindset, two undoubtedly essential elements. Now it's time to explore the last piece of the puzzle: our physiology. Although Part IV is titled "STRONGER," this is about more than just physical strength. It's about hacking our own biochemistry to improve our performance.

I promise I'm not straying into some sci-fi realm or advocating the use of performance-enhancing drugs (or any drugs for that matter!). As with everything about becoming *Unashamedly Superhuman,* it turns out that what you need to improve physical performance is the right strategies. Tapping into physiology is packed full of them but there is a caveat, one size fits one!

All the gear and no idea – that was me when I started my IRONMAN® triathlon adventure. If I was going to crash and burn, blaming my equipment was not going to be an option. As I've said, I was in desperate need of every ounce of advantage. Tapping into potential, mindset and physiology aside, I wasn't going to be let down by the kit. Fortunately, there aren't that many moving parts. Posh bike, decent pair of running shoes and some goggles should do it. I started small and went shopping for the fanciest pair of swimming goggles on the market. They're called the Magic 5. Their marketing slogan enticed me in. *One size fits one.* Once you hand over the cash you're instructed to download an app. You're then instructed to switch on your phone's camera and hold it up to your face. The extremely clever software then scans the contours of your face and sends the results to the manufacturers. Two weeks later, the coolest looking goggles arrive made to measure, just for you. The perfect fit. I can't think of a better metaphor to describe the way I'd like you to approach the final section of *Unashamedly Superhuman.*

"Tapping into Physiology" focuses on some fundamentals that will explore how to challenge your beliefs about just how strong you are. One chapter, in particular, has the potential to be divisive at best: Chapter 17, "Big Three to Thrive." Barbed wire topics at the best of times. However, I'll do the best I can. I'll talk facts and I'll back it up with my own results, but they are just that, mine.

I'll cover some breakthrough concepts that I learned from some extraordinary people that blew my mind and transformed my physiological capabilities that I believe anyone can benefit from, but I will always encourage you to run your own experiments and judge by your own results, which ultimately is the only thing that counts. I'm excited to share them with you but be prepared to challenge your beliefs about what you're capable of. Above all, be prepared to swim against the current.

> *You are braver than you believe, stronger than you seem and smarter than you think.*

> — A.A.Milne

My daughter sent me this shortly after I announced I was taking on the IRONMAN® triathlon challenge. If she couldn't hear the doubt in my voice, she most definitely picked up on the fear in my eyes. I referred back to that text on many, many occasions over the following three years.

Chapter 15

HABIT STACKING

"Starting next Monday, I will run three times a week, inject some cold into my daily shower, and only eat toast on the weekend." Experience will tell us that forming new and empowering habits is easier said than done. However, like you, I love to learn new ways to "hack" my life, and in this chapter we test, dare I say it, a fail-safe process for forging the winning habits that produce superhuman results.

There are two distinct elements of habit formation. First is breaking what we feel to be bad habits, and the second involves forming what we feel are new and improved habits. In this chapter we focus specifically on a process of adopting new ways of operating. We introduce a process that will help you to condition the behaviours that you feel will help to achieve the goals you've set yourself. In this section of *Unashamedly Superhuman*, "Tapping into Physiology," we look at things like sleep, nutrition, exercise, the benefits of cold exposure, and adoption of respiratory protocols to name a few. I'm going to use these to explain the model, but the habit formation process can be applied to any behaviours that you may wish to introduce into your life.

Habit Stacking: Align emotion and logic, then turbo charge with brain chemicals

Let's begin with the pain-pleasure principle.

> Question: When is the optimum time to wash your cereal bowl? Answer: Immediately following the consumption of said cereal.

Nowadays we all have dishwashers but before, in your student days, did you ever finish your breakfast, take your bowl to the kitchen sink and instead of immediately swilling the bowl, which would have been a 10-second job at most, you'd pause and think, "I'll come back to that, and leave the bowl for later?" How easy was it later to get those dried-on cornflakes off the side of the bowl, with a chisel?

Or do you have one of those drawers in your house that's just full of stuff? You know the one, it's often in the kitchen. Batteries, elastic bands, felt pens, expired passports. Have you ever gone to *the drawer* full of good intentions to clear it out and just as you slide it open and take a look inside a thought pops into your head, "Yeah I'll come back to that."

It's like kids and their homework. Well, maybe not all kids (although if I'm honest me when I was one). Leaving school on Friday afternoon with an essay to write for Monday. When is the optimum time to get it done? Exactly, Friday evening. Get it out of the way and enjoy the weekend. When would I actually get it done? Sunday evening of course. The interesting phase is the moment of transition, where an invisible switch is flicked that would take me from procrastination to motivation. Until that moment, literally everything else is more enjoyable than writing the essay. Kids will insist on watching *Songs of Praise* rather than get out their books. And they'll pretend to enjoy it too. Singing along enthusiastically to the "Lord Is My Shepherd." There's not a child on the planet who enjoys *Songs of Praise*, unless they have homework to do.

But at some point the switch is flicked and we're off, books open and heads down. What happens in that magic moment? Well, what happens is the pain-pleasure balance reverses itself. We go from experiencing pain at the thought of doing the homework and gaining pleasure from just about anything else, to the exact opposite. The thoughts turn to what will happen if we don't do the essay. How embarrassing will it be when the teacher asks for our work. Having to explain the *F* grade when we get home. As soon as we fully associate to the pain of not taking action, we also start to associate to the pleasure of getting the job done. The belief system that drives us now is, it *must* be done not it *should* be done. We're all fully aware of the things we should do more of in the pursuit of our goals. I should eat better, I should exercise more, I should make that call, I should start that project, I should complete my morning routine. The problem is, 'shoulds' never lead to the empowering habits we're searching for. If anything, we end up just shoulding all over ourselves! It's the musts that get things done. Taking conscious control of the pain-pleasure balance is the important first step.

The performance hack "Win Learn Change" that came from the Boris Becker story in Chapter 8 provided a pragmatic approach to evaluating our performance, but more importantly it also offered a way to rewire the feeling of failure and transition into a state of learning. When it comes to developing new habits, it's important to recognise that what has been wired in can be re-wired. What has been conditioned can be reconditioned.

I mentioned that adopting this win, or learn how to win, approach had a significant impact on my early sales career. Although I had been motivated to expand my client base I had an undeniable fear of rejection. Rejection equals failure and failure equals pain, and our nervous system is wired to avoid pain. The most skillful strategy for addressing this internal conflict is to adjust our pain/pleasure associations. Motivation didn't change my association of pain to rejection but watching the Becker interview stopped that automatic association by flipping the meaning of failing into that of receiving constructive feedback. Pain into pleasure.

There are two simple and somewhat obvious questions that can start the re-engineering process. First, what are the consequences of not developing this new habit? What do you stand to lose and how does that make you feel? Second, what are all the expected benefits of this new way of behaving? What is your win and how does that make you feel?

The fact is it's unlikely we'll follow a path to a goal if the associations are predominantly painful. For example, let's take the January 1 classics. If my goal is to lose weight, which will likely require regular exercise to which I associate pain, I may well buy all the gear and start the programme, but I'm unlikely to still be at it a month later. I'll find it all too easy to convince myself that the whole thing is just an inconvenience. "I just don't have enough time," is typically where it all ends. Generally speaking, in life most of us will opt for the choice that brings pleasure and helps us to avoid pain. In fact, it's not even actual pain and pleasure that drives us; we've mentioned before that the empowering dopamine or the stressful cortisol is released as a result of our anticipation of something happening. We're not driven by reality, but our perception of reality, and herein lies the opportunity.

So, we've taken ourselves through the pain-pleasure questions. Pain if we don't and pleasure if we do, perfectly balanced. Our emotions are in check. Next up is logic. What else can we do to make doing this behaviour even easier? Specifically, is there anything we can change in our environment to remove any friction during the transitional phase between the old behaviour and the new more desirable one? It's important to recognise that just because it's our new choice, we've been very used to not doing it, so in the first week or so we must grease the wheels of change. Therefore, how can we redesign our environment to make our commitments easier to bump into? Simple and obvious things like laying out our exercise kit and preparing sports drinks and any required nutrition the night before a planned 6 a.m. run. Subscribing to a healthy meal delivery box removes the nutrition strain and delivers everything we need for the week to encourage us to start the process of healthy eating. You get the idea. And then make it easier and stickier by using accountability apps or buddy up with a friend or colleague who's working on forging the exact same winning habit.

So, we've looked at aligning logic and emotion, but now things get really interesting. I believe this next hack is the difference that makes the difference. Factoring this in will allow you to engage in particular habits more easily and to consolidate those habits more quickly as well as make it far more likely that you'll be able to regularly engage in these behaviours over a long period of time. We're going to add in the all-important brain chemicals.

This hack involves dividing the day into two phases. Most people go to sleep somewhere around 10 p.m. plus or minus two hours and wake up sometime around 7 a.m. plus or minus two hours. There are, of course, exceptions to that rule (night shift workers, for example), but it's the phase of the day that is important in relation to the time you get up. So, the first phase is zero to eight hours after waking up, let's say between 7 a.m. and

3 p.m.; and the second phase is nine to 14 hours after you wake, so 4 p.m. to 9 p.m.

We've talked a lot about the impact of having an optimum amount of dopamine and adrenaline in our system, in particular, to increase drive and energy. Both of these chemicals tend to be higher during that first half of the day.

As a result, you are more able to engage in activities that have a high degree of friction. This is particularly helpful if the desired habit are things like strenuous exercise or cold showers or ice baths.

During the first phase, your mind and body are action- and focus-oriented, and because of the neurochemicals that are naturally released in your brain and body, you will be more likely to overcome any emotional friction that stands in the way of performing these particular activities.

So, as you list out the various habits that you'd like to adopt, take those that you believe are the hardest for you to engage in, and put them in this zero to eight hours after waking phase.

The second phase of the day turns out to be useful for acquiring other types of habits. During this phase, the amount of dopamine and adrenaline that's circulating in our brain and body tends to come down and serotonin is starting to rise, generating a more relaxed state of being. The second half of the day is more conducive for taking on things that require very little override of emotional friction. So that might be learning to play a musical instrument or another language, something that's challenging, but doesn't require all of our energy to override the initial friction of adopting new behaviours.

Running your own experiment.

OK, so how long does it take to form a new habit? Well, there is a lot of conflicting data on that one, but the number that presents itself more often than not is 21 days, so let's use that and put it into our system.

A 21-day system that relates to the formation of new and improved habits

This involves setting out to perform up to five new habits a day, across the course of 21 days. The idea is you write down five things that you would like to do every day for 21 days. However, the expectation is that you'll only complete three or four of them each day. So, built into this is a permission to fail, but it's not failure because it turns out that this approach to forming habits is based not so much on the specific habits that you're trying to form, but the habit of performing habits. So, you start on day one by writing down the five things you'd like to have as a more permanent feature in your life.

It could be a mix of activities, some easy to adopt along with those that require a bit more focus and determination. Right now much of my time and focus is taken up with blocks of writing, and as a result I've let a few things slip. So currently my list looks like this:

1.   Two X active recovery breaks
2.   SuperGreen smoothie
3.   60 minutes of cardio exercise
4.   Cold shower
5.   Win Learn Change journal entry

This isn't my "things to do" list. That's a lot more granular and typically more work-related, and of course it changes daily. This is simply a daily nudge of some supporting behaviours that I want to become second nature.

Here is a bonus hack to slam dunk this process. Rather than seeing this as a 21-day challenge, break it down into three-day sets. The proverbial "How do you eat an elephant? Bite size chunks." Just for the next three days, commit to making these choices a priority. Consciously plug them into your day. And remember the bonus ingredient to this bonus hack – if you have a day when you don't perform all six there is no punishment, you just get right back on the horse and go again the next day. After three days, take five minutes to review your wins, learns, and changes, then wipe the slate clean and crack on with the next three-day set. Then after 21 days, ask yourself how many of those particular habits that you were deliberately trying to engage in are now automatically incorporated into your schedule? How many of them are you naturally doing? Then, and only if you fancy it, run it again for another 21 days, but be careful not to have too much fun!

Emotion, logic, and brain chems aligned. Happy habit stacking.

Chapter 16

ACTIVE RECOVERY

Do you wear a Whoop strap on your wrist or perhaps a Fitbit, Apple, or Garmin? Maybe your tracking device of choice is the Oura Smart Ring? Or perhaps you see such wearables as unnecessary devices that do nothing more than cause paralysis by analysis. Well, if having your biometrics at the tip of your fingers is for you, you're not on your own. The number of connected wearable devices worldwide has more than doubled in the space of three years, increasing from 325 million in 2016 to 722 million in 2019.[1] The number of devices is forecast to reach more than one billion by the end of 2022. The general idea is they can leverage your biometric data to provide a visual reminder of your health status. It can provide you with timely and vital information to inspire healthy lifestyle choices for long-term benefits. Usually worn as wristbands, they measure the wearers' unique health information, such as their pulse, heart rate, oxygen level, and blood pressure. As you can imagine, such devices are extremely popular with sportspeople, both professional and amateur enthusiasts.

For what it's worth, I'm a fan, although not for any of the preceding reasons. I wear my Whoop strap for one reason, and one reason only, and it has absolutely nothing to do with sport.

I mentioned at the start of the book that peak performers do two things, they push themselves to the edge of their abilities and then they recover in a world-class way.

Let's just focus on the second part. They recover in a world-class way! That might sound obvious, especially if you are looking at performance through the lens of a professional athlete. If athletes push themselves physically, there comes a point when

[1] Newsmantraa, (2022), "Haptic Technology Market Growth—CAGR of 12% | Industry Trends – Advancements in Technology | Texas Instruments, Johnson Electric, AAC Technologies, TDK," *Digital Journal*, 24 March. Available at: https://www.digitaljournal.com/pr/haptic-technology-market-growth-cagr-of-12-industry-trends-advancements-in-technology-texas-instruments-johnson-electric-aac-technologies-tdk#:~:text=For%20instance%2C%20according%20to%20the,than%20one%20billion%20by%202022.

their performance will suffer if they don't replenish the glycogen stores in their muscles and allow their body to restore itself. When I bought mine, I thought that was why I wore it. In fact, when I started to train for the triathlon, I made a point of seeking the counsel of seasoned IRONMAN® athletes (both male and female). I asked, "If you could give me only one piece of advice, what would it be?" The replies were many and varied, but by far the most consistent pearl of wisdom was this: "Focus on your recovery at least as much as you focus on your performance." I even bought a book on the subject, Mark Devine's, *Unbeatable Mind.* In it he says, "the necessity not luxury of recovery." If I needed any more convincing, I watched a fascinating podcast where Joe Rogan interviewed Alex Honnold. If ever there was someone who could lay claim to superhuman status it would be Alex Honnold. *Free Solo* is a film depicting how he attempts to conquer the first free solo climb of famed El Capitan's 3,000-foot (914-km) vertical rock face at Yosemite National Park, and he's not using ropes! The billboard states:

Alex Honnolds free solo climb of El Capitan should be celebrated as one of the greatest athletic feats of any kind, ever — The New York Times

Another passage can be written in the annals of human achievement — The New Yorker

When Joe asked him, "Is there such a thing as a performance-enhancing drug in your sport?" I was keen to hear his answer. It was a great question because to perform under such intense life-and-death circumstances where the slightest mistake would be fatal, he needs to be in the perfect state of arousal. Not enough focus could lead to complacency, whilst being too amped would be equally disastrous. He thought for a moment and said, "Only if it could help speed up my recovery." I was sold. Whoop strap ordered. I'm not technically minded so I won't attempt to explain the details of the device. Let's just say, it's extremely clever! From what I can gather, when you're sleeping it calculates how much of the previous day you spent taking energy out of your tank versus how much you put in. Then when you wake it gives you a recovery score out of 100. Based on that score, the idea is that you adjust your training to suit. So, if the recovery score was, say, 75 percent it would give the following advice: *Whoop calculates how recovered your body is by measuring changes in your heart rate variability, resting heart rate, respiratory rate, and duration of sleep. Your body is recovered and ready for strain.*

If the score was 20 percent it would advise against taking on strain and instead focus on recovery. Of course, we can ignore the advice, and frankly some mornings I feel better than Whoop suggests and I do, but over time ignoring the data would likely catch up with us in the form of injuries, illness, or maybe even burnout. Anyway, so far so good, it was all making sense.

But then one morning something revelatory happened. I woke up at 6 a.m., made tea, and checked my Whoop data. It was one of those rare mornings when I was looking forward to heading to the lake for an hour's swim with the intention of then hopping on the bike for a couple of testy hours in the saddle. That was until my recovery readout read 12 percent. Even though I felt pretty good, it made me think twice. I checked my sleep stats. Not bad, a good seven hours. How come my recovery score was so low? Then my confusion kicked up a level when I reflected on the previous day. I hadn't exercised. Nothing. I hadn't even left the house. Clearly the thing was faulty.

Another feature on the device is that it tells you how many activities you engaged in the previous day that caused you strain. I checked. It said two, and the strain ratings were the equivalent of a couple of two-hour runs. And then it dawned on me. The day before I'd spoken at two conferences. A speech at 10 a.m. and another at 2 p.m. Both virtual and both delivered as I sat on a stool in my office. The a-ha moment that followed made the monthly subscription to Whoop well worth the investment. The reason I wear a fitness tracking device is to monitor my mental and emotional fitness more than it is for the physical benefits.

I don't want to over-complicate what, on the face of it, is a straightforward topic, so instead of talking in depth about the autonomic nervous system and how it's split into two parts (the sympathetic and parasympathetic, the first being active when we're in an alert and stressed state and the second when we're calm and in a relaxed state), let's just say that all day long we're doing things that either charge or drain our battery.

Turns out that when I was on my stool delivering the speeches, although I wasn't spending any physical energy, I was nevertheless draining my batteries. Any situation we're in that combines the following three ingredients: importance, uncertainty, and judgment will elevate a stressful situation into a high-pressure one. In my example, the outcome of the speech is important to me. I don't know for sure how the audience is going to react, and afterwards I will be judged either by participants' feedback or by my own standards. When we're under pressure, our mind and body respond to help us rise to the challenge. The Whoop data confirmed that my heart rate was running at over 100 beats per minute for the duration of both speeches, precisely the same as it would be if I was out for a two-hour run. I'd drained my batteries, but I hadn't done anything to recharge them. My recovery score had confirmed the fact. Imagine being oblivious to that data and running that same pattern, day in and day out, for weeks, months, or even years.

The thing is, our sympathetic nervous system is always on, expending energy, ensuring we're ready to respond to the demands of our day, whether that be positively by sharpening our focus and provoking us into flow or negatively hurling us into a state of fight or flight. The point being, we're good at it. It requires no effort. However, switching over to the restorative, parasympathetic system must be a proactive choice. Recovery paradoxically takes conscious effort!

Of course, this isn't news to us, we're fully aware of the need to recover but for many of us our recovery strategy is reactive. With good intentions we work flat out all day, and our recovery comes when we collapse in front of the TV in the evening. Or we push ourselves hard all week, and then crash and burn on the weekend.

So, what's the solution? How can we continue to push ourselves whilst at the same time recover in a world-class way? It would appear that the difference lies in both how and when we recover.

First, recovery can be broken down into two types: active recovery and micro recovery. Active recovery is any activity that is restorative and rejuvenating. Those activities that are designed to put gas back in the tank. Of course, intuitively we know how to. Whenever I pose the question at a conference, "How can you boost your mood in 20 minutes or less?" the answers come flooding in. A walk in nature is a favourite for many. If that's not on our doorstep, putting on some chilled tunes perhaps. Meditation for some; breathwork for others. Exercise, pottering in the garden, an uplifting chat with friends. Throwing a ball for the dog or sitting outside with your drink of choice and just watching the world go by.

Micro recovery includes techniques that rapidly enable us to reset and decompress. An ex-special forces colleague told me how they were trained to rapidly restore balance by switching from the sympathetic to the parasympathetic nervous system.

There were two techniques in particular. One of them is a simple breathing technique called the 4-7-8 technique (also known as "relaxing breath"). Breathe in through the nose for the count of four, hold for seven and exhale through the mouth for a count of eight. Repeat that pattern for a minute or two. It turns out when we inhale, it stimulates the stress response and when we exhale it triggers a resting state. When you think about it that makes sense. If we're suddenly startled, our instinct is to take a sharp intake of breath. We then hold our breath momentarily while we assess the potential danger. It's not until we exhale that the tension subsides. You'll remember from our session on stress-busting, Professor Huberman's rapid destress technique involved the double inhale followed by an elongated exhale.

That sigh, as he called it, expels excess carbon dioxide triggering the release of stress. The old adage, "Take a few deep breaths," should read, "Take a few deep breaths but exhale for longer than you inhale."

The second micro recovery technique is another amazing way to quickly recover composure in the heat of the moment. Imagine you're out on the plains of Africa and you see in the distance a lion. It would likely trigger a neutral response providing it's a long, long way away. We can see a broad panorama of information. We put the problem into perspective. No immediate threat. Our heart rate doesn't change too much. The brain activity would be largely in our thinking brain (the prefrontal cortex for the enthusiasts), the area of the brain that deals with planning, assessing, and generating a range of options. No fight or flight, just pause.

Compare that to turning a corner and being confronted by the lion, 10 feet in front of you. Now that's a game-changer! If you saw that, your pupils would immediately dilate. You would zone in on the potential threat. Automatically it would demand 100 percent of your attention. Everything else would become insignificant. Now the only thing you would pay attention to is the lion. No more pausing. Time to retreat. Flight mode, while you can! Your heart rate increases as blood gets redirected to the big muscles in the legs. You're not thinking consciously at this point. Your frontal cortex shuts down and all of the brain activity is now centred in the reptilian brain and our survival mechanism kicks in.

OK, that may be a bit extreme, so let's say you're about to walk on stage to give an important presentation or you've got a really difficult client call to make. Any situation that makes your heart race and palms sweat would benefit from a technique that rapidly calms a busy mind. This technique will immediately activate the part of the nervous system that engages the logical brain. It helps the mind, body, and emotions come back into balance enough, at least, to enable a conscious response rather than a knee-jerk reaction. It's called the peripheral vision exercise.

Look at the wall opposite you and find a point straight ahead and a little above eye level. While keeping your focus on that point, start to become aware of the things in the room in your peripheral vision. Notice what is off to the left and right. Don't take your eyes off the point ahead but also start to notice what's above you and on the floor. Your focus will soften as you extend your awareness to everything around you, from nine o'clock to three o'clock without moving your eyes. After a few seconds you will be paying attention to the details that you can see at the margins of your awareness, perhaps expanding past 180 degrees. Your breathing will automatically slow and your muscles will relax naturally.

I know it sounds too good to be true. How can something so simple be so effective at resetting our stress response, and how is it we weren't taught this at school? It's even better to do it outside, particularly if there is a distant horizon and a big sky. From a scientific perspective, it's one of the reasons taking a walk in nature is so relaxing. Taking in much more visual information communicates to the fight-or-flight part of the brain that we're aware of the environment around us and therefore fully aware that there is no threat to worry about. Essentially that there's no need to activate a stress response. It only takes a couple of minutes. You're literally taking control of the autonomic nervous system. A client of mine told me how she had a dental appointment on the same day that I introduced her to this simple hack. She said she was sitting in the chair, palms sweating, heart racing, and she thought, I wonder? She closed her eyes and imagined being up a mountain looking out over a vast landscape. It still worked!

The first time I tested this technique, I was also in an unlikely setting. I'd attended a tremendous programme with the Flow Research Collective called Zero to Dangerous, a comprehensive programme exploring all things Flow. I was assigned a personal coach, Brent Hogarth. Among other things, Brent had also completed an Ironman, and I was asking how I could access this super productive state while training for my upcoming event. In particular, I was struggling to relax into cold-water lake swimming. Banging out lap after lap in the comfort of a heated pool with lane markings was no preparation for the unfamiliar and challenging environment provided by Mother Nature, especially in the middle of winter. I found it almost impossible to relax into it and therefore I had zero control over perhaps the most fundamental element in any endurance event, my breathing. Trying to think our way into a composed state when the alarm bells are ringing in the fight-or-flight system is not easy. Brent advised me to simply factor in more visual stimuli as I turned my head to the side during the recovery breath. Allowing my peripheral vision to notice the sky, the tree line, and the quality of light, significantly reduced the intensity. It helped me balance the time spent in the sympathetic and parasympathetic nervous systems, thereby regulating my breathing and provoking a calm but focused state of mind. The impact was immediate, and it enabled me to de-stress and get into the all-important rhythm required for long-distance swimming.

So, that answers the question of how we can recover, but when it comes to our performance the more important question is when?

Prevention is better than cure

The recommendation to us, from those in the know, is not to wait for the alarm bells to go off in the first place. American philosopher William James said that the single most important success factor is to make our nervous system our ally instead of our enemy.

When researching this particular recovery hack, I came across a number of recommendations for its use. The data suggest that proactively injecting a little downtime into our day will keep our internal charge up.

Performance Hack: Something for Nothing

For example, if we're sitting at our desk, for hours on end, try the 20-20-20 method. Every 20 minutes look at something 20 feet away for 20 seconds. Alternatively, if you can get outside, there's the 60-60-60 version. Every 60 minutes step outside and look at something 60 feet away for 60 seconds. I guess what they are saying is that giving yourself permission to do nothing, in this instance, does in fact do something!

This idea of scheduling recovery time before we feel we need it has a lot of traction in the high-performance literature of late. If we go back to the world of endurance sports for a moment, it's long been understood that if you wait until you're thirsty before taking a drink you've blown it. Dehydration has already set in. It's now a case of too little too late. How about we take the same approach to managing our mental fitness as we do our physical fitness?

To wrap up this chapter, I'd like to share with you the opinions of a panel of three people whom I had the great pleasure to interview just as we were nearing the end of 2021. The high-performance panel consisted of Mandy Hickson, one of the UK's first female fighter pilots and author of *An Officer Not a Gentleman*; Phil Jones, Managing Director of the tech firm Brother; and Great Britain's Olympic gold-medal winning field hockey team captain Kate Richardson-Walsh. I specifically mention the date in order to take you back to the mood in the room. Around 1,000 people were in the audience and on the back of possibly the most physically and mentally draining period of our lives. I started the interview by asking them how they had not just coped, but thrived during such a demanding time. Their answers are inspiring.

Phil talked about staying calm in a crisis. CALM refers to Communication, Action orientation, Level headedness, and being Mindful about every decision that you make. He said that to look after those around you, you have to look after yourself. To do so, he had another great acronym which he called his DESK policy: diet, exercise, sleep, and kindness to self. The first three we'll be digging into in the next chapter. His take on self-care was both insightful and pragmatic. He said that recovery was a component of optimum performance.

This reminded me of the quote I started this chapter with: recover in a world-class way. Before my *recovery percentage a-ha moment,* I doubt I was the only person to think that taking a recovery break was a bit of a cop-out. Plenty of time to sleep when you're dead, right? I'd certainly never connected taking a time out as a high-performance strategy. I put that to our resident athlete. Kate said that as professional athletes, of course, she and her team would push themselves every day to their limit, but at times the focus was only on recovering their bodies, not recovering their minds. She went on to say how they proactively built that into their programme.

For example, on a Friday they had a *give back to yourself day.* They were actively encouraged to do something that was good for them. She said that initially it felt really selfish, but they quickly realised that to be the best for the team on game day they needed to be resting their mind as well as their body. It formed part of their team culture and, in her opinion, was one of those winning differences.

As someone who now runs her own business, Mandy added a different context. She highlighted how easy it is for our days to creep onto our evenings and our weeks into our weekends. *Just one more email* and suddenly you've lost three hours. "I realised that was me and so I really delineated weekdays and weekends," she said. She went on to say how she loved reading so made the decision to sit down and say, "This is going to be my holiday time, and I literally read a book every weekend. Most important of all, we need to accept and acknowledge that as part of our high-performance regime." There it was again.

I think it is important for us to realise that people who are trying to be successful do take time out. There's this misnomer

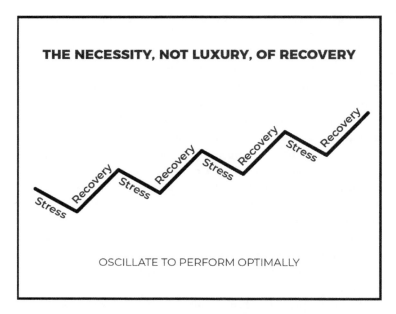

Figure 16.1 Oscillation = optimal performance

that it's just flat out, 24/7. The model that neuroscientists talk about is called oscillating (see Figure 16.1).

This recognises that stress is inevitable. In fact, some might say it's not the stress that'll get you, it's the lack of recovery. The lack of active recovery brings us down. That would involve alternating periods of high stress with short bursts of recovery, such as planning a micro hack between calls or scheduling a couple of 20-minute active recovery breaks during the day. Effectively we're planning decompression time inbetween our bouts of productive activity. It's important to differentiate between recovery and recuperation. This isn't about long-term recuperation; we've got holidays for that. This is about adopting daily practices that ensure that when we get to our holidays, we've got the energy to do more than fry ourselves face-down on our beach towel.

I'll leave the last word to Phil. His final comments really hit home. He told the room that as he was going through his career it had all been about working all the hours God gave, but there came a point when he realised that was only getting him so far. "I had an interest in bridging over to become a senior executive and I realised that you can only rev so far before you rev out and there comes a point when you've got to be able to change it up a gear. The strategy that made the difference was strategically scheduling breaks into the day." He added, "It's okay to have a little walk. It's okay to just go out and have a breather to change your dynamics and change your energy. Give yourself personal permission so that your energy levels can be appropriate for the next task ahead." Enough said!

Chapter 17

BIG THREE TO THRIVE

The time in a day may be fixed, but the amount of energy available is variable and elite performance is a function of the skillful management and mobilisation of your energy.

— *Michael Gervais*

Sleep

Whether talking to successful business people or professional athletes, the doctors who advise them on energy management say, over and over, that the No. 1 strategy for recovery, more than exercise, nutrition, or literally anything else, is a good old-fashioned night's sleep. I have to be honest, this is another of those areas that I'm working on. I can't argue with the data. My Whoop data considers me to be a poor sleep performer. Sounds crazy now, knowing what we know about the benefits of sleep, or perhaps more importantly the consequences of not getting enough, but I'd never really connected sleep with performance.

However, it turns out that being under-slept is far worse than we tend to think. Work done at King's College London, John Hopkins, and University of California, Berkeley found that a lack of quality sleep contributes to a wide range of issues over and above the consequence of struggling to get into first gear without a third coffee.

A deep dive for a deep sleep

So, how do high-performing sleepers do it? Let's begin with sleep hygiene 101. This is the stuff we've all heard a million times, but once again, just because it's common sense doesn't mean it's our common practice.

So, make sure your room is cool and totally dark. Not eating less than two hours before bed and doing some early evening exercise will all help. Nothing new there. Makes sense and is easy to do. Not so easy, but worth a mention, is no caffeine after 3 in the afternoon, no alcohol after 7 p.m., and chop out the phone scrolling at least 30 minutes before lights out. Who knew sleeping would require such discipline?

Good sleep "performers" seem to have a good routine to wind down before bed. Apparently one of the most effective strategies is to have a consistent "Go to and get up time." Same time every time. Sounds obvious, but when so many of our routines have changed during the day, it can have a knock-on effect on our sleep patterns. So, if it's the classic eight hours that you need in order to bounce out of bed in the morning, ready and raring to go at 7 a.m., it's lights out at 11 p.m. Tonight and almost every night.

Good sleepers also recommend closing all open "cognitive loops" or clearing your mind before lights out. We've mentioned this before, taking just five minutes to think ahead to the following day and writing down your main priorities. Just your top two or three goals and a short clear *to do list* is a great way to reduce any unnecessary over-thinking. So, those are the basics and maybe already part of your routine. But, this is *Unashamedly Superhuman*. We need more than just the basics.

How about napping? Are you a napper? I've never been a napper. I love the idea of it, but I struggle with it. I think it's called FOMO (fear of missing out)! However, I read in an article in *Harvard Business Review*[1] that napping is the new performance-enhancing drug! The article started with the question: "Who says a lunchtime recharge is just for infants and kindergartners?" It claimed that mid-day naps can improve your mood and boost productivity, well-being, and performance. And it said, "If you're one of the many who wish they could step away from the desk and catch 40 winks, then you're in good company." Some of history's greatest minds and high performers have shared your sentiment and used naps as a way to help them get the job done. Winston Churchill is perhaps one of the most well-known nappers.

The science confirms that our body repairs and rebuilds while we're asleep, physically and mentally. So give it an extra

---

[1] Barnes, C.M., (2018), "Sleep Well, Lead Better," *Harvard Business Review*, September–October issue, pp. 140–143.

boost with a 10–20 minute power down. Margaret Thatcher was another napper. "The Iron Lady" was famously known for working 20-hour days. But to ensure she was running on all cylinders, she would take short snooze breaks during the day to make up for her less than restful nights.

Leonard da Vinci apparently had a very irregular sleeping pattern too. He took 15-minute naps every four hours. Another creative and innovative napper was the artist Salvador Dali. He took afternoon naps that were designed to last no longer than one second. One second! I know you're too busy to nap, but we can all spare one second. Albert Einstein was also a fan of what people call a micro nap. Both Dali and Einstein would sit in a chair and hold a metal key or a pen. Then the moment they dropped off, it would drop to the floor and wake them up. Both believed this short nap fired up their mind and body. Genius. Difficult to argue with these heavyweight sleep performers.

However, if you're just not good at it, and I'm not, where do we start? Of course some of the mindfulness practices, in particular, meditation, can be helpful, but if they still sound a bit woo-hoo for you, there is a particularly practical and science-based option that you could try. It's called Yoga Nidra. No navel gazing, just deliberate disengagement. Not trying to fall asleep. Not trying to meditate. Just deliberately disengaging from any planning and doing, except breathing.

Yoga Nidra literally means yoga sleep. You lie down and listen to a script. When I started meditating I found it difficult to do over a long period and I also didn't know if I was doing it right, whereas with Yoga Nidra it's quick, pleasant, and impossible to get wrong. Ten to 30 minutes replenishes circuits of the brain that enable people to be more efficient in their actions afterwards. It's pseudo sleep. The rationale is that a lot of people have trouble sleeping and dealing with stress. Their nervous system is on a state of high alert for too much of the day. Here, we are teaching ourselves to calm our nervous system quickly.

Also people who do Yoga Nidra regularly find they have an easier time falling and staying asleep at night.

The most effective way to recover from a demanding, high-octane day and set us up for the opportunities that are waiting tomorrow is to get a solid eight hours, anytime during 24 hours. Sleep, nap, it all adds up. Run your own experiment and test some of these practical methods from this deep dive into a deep sleep.

Nutrition

"By replacing your morning coffee with green tea, you can lose up to 87 percent of what little joy you still have left in your life."

Before I start this section on nutrition, and in the interest of transparency, I feel compelled to make a confession. Forgive me reader for I have sinned. It's 1.52 p.m. and I've just dispatched a mountain of chips, a large piece of fried cod, and a portion of mushy peas. There's more. On the way home from the chippy, I had a sausage in batter for the journey. Large! Considering it's Tuesday lunchtime I probably shouldn't mention the large glass of wine that I paired it with. I feel lighter for telling you, although obviously not literally. Joking aside, we don't have to be overly obsessive, but if we desire an endless supply of energy it would be worth considering the following.

Better living through chemistry still requires better living

Energy production naturally refers to more than just our ability to run farther. It relates to any activity that requires us to keep driving forward. Pushing ourselves to the edge of our abilities on a daily basis for an extended shift at our desk equally requires a strategy for sustained levels of endurance. Resilience and endurance will no doubt be impacted by our fuel utilisation. We've already looked at a number of things, aside from nutrition, that can support a world-class endurance strategy. We've looked at how activating our seeking system with clear and inspiring goals triggers dopamine that suppresses the quit reflex, enabling a greater level of persistence. We've also explored how accessing flow states boosts a whole range of brain chemistry that supports forward movement, and how planning in active recovery through oscillation can sustain us through long bouts of activity. All of the preceding have a strong dotted line to generating and maintaining the energy needed to take our performance to new levels.

But this section is specifically focused on nutrition, which I'm sure we'd all agree is a fundamental building block for energy. When I started writing this chapter, I was interested to see what my position would be on the subject. It's a complex topic and one that I'd never really made my priority, at least not until I took on the gargantuan physical challenge of completing 140 miles (225 km) in a day, without the assistance of my grey Audi. I was excited because, remember, I was looking for anything that would enable me to tap into new strategies gleaned from exploring uncharted territory, so this one was going to be a gold mine for me.

That said, from the outset I knew at some point I would come across information that would cause me to have to challenge my understanding of this diverse topic, let alone my current eating habits. So, if I was going to disagree with my own thoughts and ideas on the matter, what chance would there be of you and I being aligned?

This is an opportune time to remind you of the one-size-fits-one concept. Diet has to be the ultimate barbed wire question. Which diets or nutrients are best? Plant-based, omnivore, carnivore, Mediterranean, or vegan? Should we eat based on our blood type, our culture, our gender, our body shape, or perhaps we should eat nothing at all between the hours of 8 p.m. and 12 noon the following day, or some other iteration of the latest craze, intermittent fasting? See my point?

Of course, I'd be on safe ground with the basics. Nobody is going to argue with getting in your 5 A Day, avoiding processed foods, and the benefits of drinking a couple of litres (quarts) of water. I suspect we will also agree on some of the classics. Everything in moderation and a little bit of what you fancy does you good, although we've also been taught that you can have too much of a good thing.

Whatever the case may be regarding our understanding of the good and bad of our dietary intake, you and I both know that a double burger and fries wouldn't get me round the IRONMAN® triathlon. So, my approach to this thorny topic is less about the nuts and bolts of our specific diets, and more to do with the process for developing our unique nutritional strategy. I mention some of the more interesting discoveries that I came across in my search for a massive uplift in energy, but I'm not fool enough to believe that my personal strategy is a fix all for all. So, let's be clear, prescribing what you put inside your body is outside of the remit of this chapter; however, provoking the necessary research certainly isn't.

When I read that nutrition is the fourth discipline of an IRONMAN® triathlon, I was highly motivated to maximise on this glaring opportunity for establishing new performance gains. After much research and self-reflection, I decided that my strategy for nutrition would be contextual. It would be determined by one thing and one thing only: my goals. I would recommend the same. I'd also recommend that once the goal is set, be forensic about finding and testing new ideas that, above all, do one thing and that's get results.

Before I touch on the approach that I took, I want to share something on nutrition that ties into our section on mindset. This will affect the way you think about food forever. If ever there was an example to promote the case for shifting from a negative to positive mindset when it comes to our beliefs on nutrition, this is it.

Dr Alia Crum of Stanford University conducted a study in relation to our mindset about food.[2] She started by asking,

[2] Crum, A. J., Corbin, W., Brownell, K., and Salovey, P., (2011), "Mind Over Milkshakes: Mindsets, Not Just Nutrients, Determine Ghrelin Response," *Health Psychology*, July, 30(4): 424–429; discussion 430–431. doi: 10.1037/a0023467. PMID: 21574706.

"Do you have the mindset that healthy foods are good for you? Do you believe that they are depriving you of something nicer?" You might be different, but she found that people in our culture in the West generally have the view that healthy foods are less than pleasant, and those mindsets whether true or false, right or wrong, have an impact. Her point is that our attitude matters because it's shaping the way we're thinking, what we're paying attention to, what we're motivated to do, and potentially even how our bodies respond.

The study that reinforces this viewpoint was known as the Milkshake study and it emphasises the interplay between mind-set and physiology. The leading question was: Do our beliefs about what we're eating change our body's physiological response to that food? We're now getting into the realms of the placebo effect. Interestingly, she says there is more evidence on placebo effects than for any other drug because of the clinical trial process in which all new drugs and medication are required to outperform a placebo. Taking a sugar pill, under the impression that it's a real medication, has resulted in relieving asthma, reducing blood pressure, and boosting the immune system. It can lead to physiological effects. Even though there's no actual medication. So, to what degree are these things influenced by our mindsets or beliefs about them?

To test this question, Dr Crum's team ran a seemingly simple study. This was done at the Yale Center for Clinical and Translational Research, and they brought people into the lab, under the impression that they were designing different milkshakes with vastly different concentrations of nutrients. The volunteers would drink these milkshakes and their body's physiological response was measured. It was the same people consuming two different milkshakes, separated by a week. They were told that they were consuming a high-fat, high-calorie indulgent milkshake that had 620 calories. A week later they were told that it was a low-fat, low-calorie diet shake. In reality, it was the exact same shake and it was right in the middle containing 300 calories. When measuring the body's response, they were looking at the hormone ghrelin. Medical experts call this the hunger hormone. It causes us to seek out food. Theoretically, the number of calories you consume affects the ghrelin and it sends a signal to the brain telling you either to eat more or less.

What they found in this study was that when people thought they were consuming the high-fat, high-calorie indulgent milk-shake, their ghrelin levels dropped at a threefold rate more than when they thought they were consuming the sensible shake. So essentially, their bodies responded as if they had consumed more food, even though it was the exact same shake. This was one of the first studies to show that just believing what you're eating can have an impact on your physiology. Of course, this isn't saying that just believing our food is healthy makes it so.

The single most important factor for me when it came to nutrition was endurance. As I mentioned, anything that fuels our endurance for physical challenges will also support us when pushing ourselves in other areas of life, so I figured the payoff for seeking out and developing my strategy would be something that would benefit me long after the triathlon had been and gone.

I'd read that anything that promoted a steady release of energy not only prevented the highs and lows of sugar rushes, but would also have a positive effect on reducing inflammation. After all my back and knee surgeries, inflammation was one thing that I thought could cause me to grind to a halt. It's not only relevant to how I would get on during my race, but more to do with avoiding injury when training 10–15 hours a week, week in week out.

As I said, this book isn't about keeping fit, so I'm not going to go into the finer details of my strategy. I will tell you that I decided on a low-carbohydrate, high-fat adaptive approach. I'd never heard of it before, and it was most definitely a case of *swimming against the current* for me. It started off with a period in Ketosis which was challenging but wonderful. I've never been so clear of mind. It then transitions to a more manageable low-carb regime.

For those who are interested in digging into the details, I'd point you in the direction of a company called Endure IQ. As with everything else in this book, I have no affiliation to the company or authors, I just want to tell you the way it was, along with respecting those who helped me along the way. In my search for the latest, cutting-edge content on all things related to the best nutritional strategy for ultra endurance, I turned to a guy named Dan Plews. Dan runs Endure IQ, which is based at the University of Auckland and, apart from running top-notch sports nutrition courses, also provides a learning community for endurance athletes. For me, Dan was the perfect person to turn to because he's not only an applied sports scientist, researcher, and coach; he's also a World Champion IRONMAN® athlete. I believe, on this topic, that modelling someone else's excellence is a great place to start. Engage in a programme of research to create the plan that works for you. Look for people who are achieving the results you want and be prepared to swim against the current. As they say, *what has got us here, won't necessarily get us there.* If your goal has changed, then your strategy should too!

Just a note on hydration, I read somewhere that …

I found a company called Precision Fuel & Hydration who make a valid point that most of us pay little attention to how much sodium we lose during long bouts of exercise. Incredibly the amount we can lose can vary by up to 15 times from person to person. The company's website takes you through a simple sweat test and the result enables you to tailor your salt intake to suit.

I did say that I was forensic but that's nothing compared to my next hack. Recognising my limitations on sports nutrition, I decided it was time to get super scientific. This one is specific to the challenge I'd set myself, but it will demonstrate the lengths I was prepared to go to in the pursuit of cutting-edge information. I'd been watching triathlon events on TV and I'd seen that some of the athletes had something attached to their arms. A small circular device. After a bit of digging I found out that it was a product called Supersapiens. Turns out that the company that produced it not only sponsors the IRONMAN® World Championship at Kona, but its main brand ambassador was also none other than Jan Frodeno, currently the No. 1 IRONMAN® athlete in the world.

The company's marketing literature asked this enticing challenge: "Imagine going into a race knowing you will have the right energy to enable you to perform at your best."

Great thought. Without doubt, it would be one thing less to worry about. Not only a physical and mental boost, but improved confidence too, which are three boxes I was in need of ticking. Its website says that it "focuses on energy management systems to support sustained peak performance." It went on to note that, "Supersapiens empower athletes to show up to the starting line optimally fuelled, manage in-race fuelling to sustain peak performance, and adequately refuel and recover." I was sold.

The Supersapiens system works via a biosensor, which is a small patch that sticks to the back of your upper arm. It has a thin, flexible filament that inserts just under the skin to access your interstitial fluid. This fluid surrounds the cells of the tissues just below your skin and by analysing it, the device can measure your glucose levels in real time. As has been mentioned, the challenge with nutrition is that there's no single strategy that works for everyone. You can read endless scientific journals or get expert advice, but ultimately you still must apply trial and error to find out what works for you.

Glucose is the body's primary source of fuel for exercise and knowing your body's glucose levels in real time means you can see exactly how your nutrition is affecting you. You can see what food works and what brands of nutrition work for you. You can avoid glucose spikes and troughs during exercise, by knowing when you need a top-up of energy and how much is required. Not only was this information critical when out training, but more importantly it provided me with a real-time programme of nutritional education. During the two weeks that I used the Supersapiens device it forced me into a steep learning curve where I got to understand everything I needed to know about what my body needed to meet the demands I was putting it under. The IRONMAN® event is since long gone, but the knowledge will support me forever.

There is no doubt in my mind, and I'm sure you'd agree, that our nutritional intake will have a significant impact on our ability to harness our inner power. The details of your own strategy for success will no doubt evolve over time, but I'd like to at least suggest my simple syntax of things to do. Start by defining your objectives. Why do you want a significant uplift in energy and endurance? What will it do for you and what are all the ways you stand to benefit? Then, once you've decided on your approach, apply the Win Learn Change performance hack that is discussed at the end of Chapter 8 for developing those ongoing marginal gains.

Finally, as Dr Alia Crum proved with her Milkshake experiment, it's essential to back your plan all the way. When you see the positive results of your nutritional choices, remind yourself that you're on the right path. If the data is anything to go by, you'll be strengthening empowering beliefs, and unconsciously getting your mind and body to work with you and not against you.

Exercise

Even for those of us with the busiest of schedules, any opportunity we have to do any exercise, at any time, is likely to be advantageous. No, not likely to be, definitely will be. A Google search will pull up hard evidence to back up this emphatic claim. In fact, I didn't need to look past the very first item on the list.

The article claims that overwhelming evidence exists that lifelong exercise is associated with a longer health span, delaying the onset of 40 chronic conditions/diseases.[3]

---

[3] Ruegsegger, G.N., and Booth, F.W., (2018), "Health Benefits of Exercise," *Cold Spring Harbor Perspectives in Medicine,* Jul 2, 8(7): a029694. doi: 10.1101/cshperspect.a029694. PMID: 28507196; PMCID: PMC6027933.

That's 40! OK, here goes. Pick out your favourite.

1. Accelerated biological ageing/premature death (I could stop there but motive is a wonderful thing.)
2. Aerobic (cardiorespiratory) fitness. VO_2 max
3. Arterial dyslipidermia
4. Balance
5. Bone fractures/falls
6. Breast cancer
7. Cognitive dysfunction
8. Colon cancer
9. Congestive heart failure
10. Constipation
11. Coronary (ischemic) heart disease
12. Deep vein thrombosis
13. Depression and anxiety
14. Diverticulitis
15. Endometrial cancer
16. Endothelial dysfunction
   Of course, by now we will have lost the 20-somethings readers. They'll have skipped this section on account of the fact that they're indestructible, which I think is fair enough; we all thought that. For the rest of us, you're doing well, *keep it up*, there may be something coming that tips the motivational balance.
17. Erectile dysfunction
18. Gallbladder diseases
19. Gestational diabetes
20. Hemostasis
21. Hypertension
22. Immunity
23. Insulin resistance
24. Large arteries lose more compliance with aging
25. Metabolic syndrome
26. Nonalcoholic fatty liver disease
27. Obesity
28. Osteoarthritis
29. Osteoporosis.

30. Ovarian cancer
31. Pain
32. Peripheral artery disease
33. Preeclampsia
34. Polycystic ovary syndrome
35. Prediabetes
36. Rheumatoid arthritis
37. Sarcopenia
38. Stroke
39. Tendons being less stiff
40. Type 2 diabetes

Alright, so we're agreed exercise is a must do, not a should do. Now what?

Again, right at the start of this section let me be clear, I'm not in a position to advise you on which specific forms of exercise you should be engaging in. I'm no fitness coach. I also realise that as soon as anyone talks about exercise or nutrition publicly, they're opening themselves up to all sorts of challenges because you can find support for almost any protocol. However, like you, I understand that if tapping into our inner superhuman is the objective, this is not a topic that can be avoided. The key word again is *objective*. As you know, to help me to get a deeper understanding of this fundamental life skill, I took on something that demanded I get to grips with it.

After nearly three years of scheduling exercise before anything else, for what it's worth, my two cents on the topic are this. Exercise is worth every minute of the effort, both for what it gives you in the moment and for what it gives you down the road. Put time into increasing your muscle mass, your strength, your cardiovascular performance, and your respiratory capability. Bottom line: if intensive, well-formulated exercise does not occupy one of our top priorities for longevity, it's time to re-examine our priorities.

Right, rant over. Let's dive into this particularly challenging but rewarding topic.

More to this one than meets the eye

Knowing what to do doesn't equal doing what we know. We've talked about motivation, and we've looked at habit stacking; both fundamental when endeavouring to factor more additional movement into our already busy schedules. However, when it comes to exercise, there's no shortcut to our own version of inner superhuman. No *hacks* in this section. We can, however, get a lot smarter when it comes to working harder.

As I mentioned in the previous section on nutrition, adopting a new approach to exercise can be made significantly easier when it's goal driven. Defining our goal should do three things: (1) clarifies what we're looking to get from our exercise habits, which (2) provides more motivation, which comes from being clear about why we're doing it, and (3) informs us how we can go about achieving the results we're looking for.

For example, let's say our goal is to climb a mountain, figuratively speaking. The overriding outcome is obvious, to reach the summit, but how we go about achieving that outcome will depend on the path we choose to take. The question to answer is: What's most important to us along the way?

If you value speed the most, that will shape your approach; however, if you decide that learning is more important, stopping along the way to discuss lessons learned will take priority. Being clear about your values hierarchy makes it much easier to make decisions. This will help you to answer questions like: which exercise is best, how much should we do, and is it important enough to us to ensure it finds its way into our schedule?

You may be familiar with the frequently used metaphor for prioritisation as the example of trying to fit big rocks, pebbles, and sand into an empty jar. If you start filling the jar by first adding sand, then pebbles, you will not have room for rocks. The big rocks symbolise the things that are the most important in our life. These are determined by having a well-formed outcome.

So, what is most important for you? Is it health, fitness, strength, endurance, body shape, energy, or maybe it's just to have fun with family or friends? Probably a combination of the preceding. For some it will be geared towards a specific event, literally a mountain to climb or some other one-off, aim-high objective, while for others it will be more of a lifestyle choice, a way of meeting their energy needs over the long term. For me it was the one-off, ultra-triathlon, and for those interested to know how that turned out I've included a couple of paragraphs at the end of this section. The upside of a single point of focus is it provides a tremendous amount of motivation to take immediate action. The downside is, it reaches a point of completion and an achieved goal no longer motivates. That's where having a life-long strategy for maintenance comes in.

There are typically two forms of exercise. The first is cardio-vascular, where the idea is to repeat a movement over and over continuously—running, biking, swimming, rowing, and the like. Cardiovascular exercise is typically more aerobic, meaning with oxygen. With breath, not out of breath. The second is resistance training where we're moving or lifting things of progressively heavier and heavier weight that you couldn't do continuously. Resistance exercise is more anaerobic.

A variation of the following practice is a great way to kick-start the day. It was prescribed to me by my fitness coach, and it con-sists of 15 minutes of breathwork, followed by just 15 minutes of any exercise. By the way, to make it a forever plan, the intensity of the exercise shouldn't exceed that which you'd look forward to doing every day for the rest of your life. Next, inject a little cold into the shower and finally give yourself 15 minutes either meditating on your day ahead, or, if that's not your vibe, take a brew of your choice and write down the answers to the three priming questions, ideally while sitting outside. Whatever exer-cise goals you set, they should inform the habits and behaviours that will support your aspiration.

Chapter 16 on active recovery made the point that we tend to get more of those things that we measure. For those high-impact and often shorter-term goals, we can often measure our success by the progress we can see in our performance. Are we getting faster, stronger, fitter, lighter, or heavier? It's not so obvious when measuring progress with our lifelong plan.

Enter the segmented body composition reading. I heard about this for the first time this morning. I've booked one at my local gym for this afternoon. A segmented body composition reading will tell you your biological age rather than your chronological age.

The body composition scale sends an imperceptible current through your body. This technology is called bioelectrical impedance analysis. Muscle, fat, bone, and water conduct electricity at different rates. These rates of resistance are measured by the monitor. The body composition monitor processes this information combined with formulas and data such as your gender and age. This provides you with a wealth of measurements.

You'll have insight into 10 different useful health measurements for the whole body. Additionally, you can measure the body fat and muscle mass percentages of your trunk and each arm and leg separately. You can use this information to spot muscle imbalances and adjust your training accordingly. Creating a training plan with a fitness professional that is focused on making your body younger as you get older is a terrific idea for ongoing lifelong motivation.

It's all in the mind. Well, some of it is

When all's said and done and you have decided on your very own plan of action, whether focusing on big goals or implementing daily disciplines, this final point will give you an extra 10-percent return on your investment, completely free of charge. We all have mindsets about exercise. Do you feel like you're getting enough or do you feel like you're getting an insufficient amount to get the health benefits you're seeking?

Ellen Langer is a professor of psychology at Harvard. She participated in a fascinating study[4] that looked at the benefits of exercise. But how do you go about testing the impact of our mindset on our exercise gains, if any? Well, she took a group of people who were getting a lot of exercise, but weren't aware of it, such as a group of hotel housekeepers. These women were working in hotels, on their feet all day long, pushing carts, changing linens, climbing stairs, cleaning bathrooms, and vacuuming. It was clear that they were getting above and beyond the recommended amount of 30 minutes of moderate physical activity per day.

Interestingly when the researchers went in and asked them how much exercise they thought they were getting the average response was a three on a scale of zero to 10, whilst a third of them said zero, *I don't get any exercise.* So, even though these women were active, they had the mindset that their work was just work; hard work that led them to feel tired and in pain at the end of the day, but not that it was good for them. So, they took the women and randomised them into two groups. Both groups had a series of physiological metrics measured like weight, body fat, and blood pressure before and after the following four-week period, after which they were tested again. Even though they hadn't changed anything in their behaviour and didn't report any changes in their diets, the group who now believed that their work was a form of positive exercise all reported feeling better about themselves, about their bodies, and about their work. The remarkable thing, however, was they all also lost weight and on average had up to a 10-point decrease in their blood pressure! Exercise has a remarkable potency, and that potency can be enhanced by believing in our fitness programme of choice. Both exercise and what you think about it matter!

---

[4] Crum, A.J., and Langer, E.J., (2007), "Mind-set Matters: Exercise and the Placebo Effect," *Psychological Science*, 18(2): 165–171.

An exercise hack after all. Do try this at home!

If you're inclined to read Chapter 20, "IRONMAN® Athlete. To Be or Not to Be That Is the Question," I'll explain my best efforts in applying everything I learned during the process of researching *Unashamedly Superhuman*. If you've already had your fill of me banging on about it, let me invite you to at least try this. If you give it a go, I guarantee your response will be something along the lines of, "What the hell just happened?"

The push-up is a strength-training staple. For this basic gym necessity, you shouldn't settle for anything other than perfect form, especially because it's such a simple, essential movement. You're not just flopping to the ground and pumping yourself up and down until you burn out; there are important aspects of the foundational plank position that you need to keep in mind every time.

A push-up isn't just a chest exercise. It's a position of full body tension. So, start in a good plank, shoulders squeezed, glutes tight, abs tight.

One of the most common push-up mistakes is trying to hollow out your back. Doing so limits your ability to move your shoulders freely, and it'll make the push-up a struggle. It can also lead to front shoulder issues because every time you push up, you're creating limited space for rotator cuff tendons to move between humerus and clavicle.

Think of squeezing a walnut between your shoulder blades as you lower into the push-up. Pull your torso to the ground, tightening those back muscles, then push up.

OK, now drop and give it your best. It doesn't matter if your best is two, 22, or 52, just focus your mind and ease out as many as you can.

Now for the magic. . .

You remember the power breathing exercise that you did at the beginning of the book?

Do exactly the same again, 30 full breaths, but this time when you exhale after the 30th one, hold with no air in your lungs and start your push-ups. Be prepared for a thoroughly pleasant surprise.

The moral of the story is: always oxygenate your body before exercising. Who says? The Iceman says, that's who.

Chapter 18

ICEMAN COMETH

We may not agree on all aspects of the big three—sleep, nutrition, and exercise, but now we're heading for calmer waters. But, brace yourself because these waters are cold, extremely cold.

Success leaves clues

I've always championed the concept of modelling excellence. Other people's experience is a treasure trove of information. In Napoleon Hill's classic self-help book, *Think and Grow Rich,*[1] the secret that he alludes to is the priceless value of building your very own mastermind alliance. In other words, having people around us, coaches, mentors, and the like, who can help us to shortcut our way to success. For example, at the height of the Renaissance, art students spent long periods copying the techniques of recognised masters. Even Michelangelo didn't think he was above this practice. When one of his fellow students asked how long they would have to go on learning in this way, Michelangelo is claimed to have said, "Until we can do it as well as they could." So, when I sat down and pulled together my plan for this book, my initial intention was to select one person for each chapter. A case study. Somebody who demonstrated the points that I wanted to raise. I drew up a list of household names. Extraordinary people who had achieved extraordinary things. Some of them I knew personally, some I'd interviewed in the

serendipity
/ˌsɛr(ə)nˈdɪpɪti/

Noun

The occurrence and development of events by chance in a happy or beneficial way.

---

[1] Hill, N., (2010), *Think and Grow Rich, Original 1937 Classic Edition,* CreateSpace Independent Publishing Platform, Reprint edition.

past, whilst others I'd just admired from afar. We're now two chapters from home, so you'll have noticed I had a significant re-think.

Two things happened. First, I had a wipe out on the bike, six weeks before IRONMAN® Copenhagen, and second, I read the front cover of Scott Carney's book *What Doesn't Kill Us*. "How Freezing Water, Extreme Altitude and Environmental Conditioning Will Renew Our Lost Evolutionary Strength." Let me explain. After making the decision to take on the IRONMAN® event as provocation to test my findings, I endeavoured to model the excellence of others and embarked on a tried and tested route to physical fitness. I chopped out the partying, cleaned up my diet, and put in the hard yards. Just 12 months later I was fitter and stronger however, although I wouldn't admit it to myself, I was nowhere near ready for the test that lay ahead. Of course, I'd still booked the flight and accommodation and I was going to go anyway and give it my best shot. My ego wouldn't have had it any other way. Would I have gotten to the finish line? Possibly. Would I have incurred any long-term damage? Highly likely. Fortunately, I never got to find out.

I didn't feel that fortunate when I woke up in the ambulance. I don't remember much about the accident other than how rapidly I went from travelling at 25 miles an hour to being face down in a ditch. I can still hear the cracking sound. I remember feeling disappointed that I'd just broken my neck and for what may lie ahead. Again, I was fortunate, my neck wasn't broken. I'm not trying to put a positive spin on the accident, but as a direct result of having to start the whole training process again, it proved to be the turning point, resulting in me finding every game-changing strategy that has made it into *Unashamedly Superhuman*. Which brings me to the second serendipitous moment. The statement on the cover of Scott Carney's book, reads, "How Freezing Water, Extreme Altitude and Environmental Conditioning Will Renew Our Lost Evolutionary Strength." It was the "renew our lost evolutionary strength" bit that gave me the belief that the IRONMAN® event was still on.

My pre accident book strategy was to suggest to the reader that the secrets for success lay in studying the extraordinary achievements of others. My post accident strategy changed to, look deeper within yourself. Encouraging the reader to tap into their own readily available, in-built Human Resources. Regular folk becoming better, smarter, and stronger in order to achieve extraordinary achievements of their own.

That's not to say that we shouldn't model the excellence of others, success does indeed leave clues, and maybe there is room to explore that in future books, but not this one. This one is about us, for us.

At this point you could challenge me. "You say you decided not to make a study of extraordinary people and yet you still included Wim Hof. He is undoubtedly extraordinary. He's even got a superhero name. The Iceman!"

It's a fair challenge.

His achievements are remarkable.

He swam under ice for 217 feet (66 metres)!

He ran a barefoot half-marathon above the Arctic Circle only wearing shorts!

He climbed Everest and Kilimanjaro in just boots and shorts!

He holds 22 Guinness world records for endurance.

However, contrary to most gurus who are promoting the promise of a stronger, happier, healthier, and more successful life, he doesn't say, be like me, or anybody else for that matter, in order to achieve what I have achieved. He doesn't say the answer is *out there* somewhere. For me, the most remarkable thing about Wim Hof is that he believes anything he can do, you can do too, and, what's more, he insists you check out the science that proves it. The Iceman! Let's take a closer look at the Iceman and his method, in particular, the two techniques that enabled him to activate his lost evolutionary strength.

He's an acquired taste. A confident, gung-ho character with remarkable self-belief. Whether or not he is your cup of tea, one thing it's hard to argue with is the science that backs up his seemingly impossible feats of endurance, and there is a tremendous amount of it. The following are just a selection of the universities and medical schools that have taken an interest in his achievements: Stanford, Imperial College London, Harvard, and Michigan, which have all *flown him in* and put him under the microscope. In laboratory conditions they tested to see how he was controlling his stress response and his physiology to adapt to the demands that the arctic conditions had to throw at him.

Initially, it was thought he was an unnaturally gifted individual, and that he had stumbled across a quirk in human physiology that dramatically impacted his ability to adapt to extreme conditions.

The question is: Can you and I hack into this quirk in human physiology and if so, how?

Many hours of digging into the weeds of peer-reviewed papers, watching umpteen podcasts of medical practitioners pouring over the findings, and more enjoyably just listening to Wim talk about his backstory provided me with enough evidence to trust in the process. More recently, Wim and his team have taken the time to collate all you could wish to know and have documented it on their website. I found the following, which dramatically proved his claim that anything he could do, we could do too.

What "The Iceman" Wim Hof is capable of was long viewed as scientifically impossible. It wasn't until the first Radbound University study in 2011 that things really kicked off. The study showed that by using his method, Wim was able to voluntarily influence his autonomic nervous system, something which until then was thought impossible. This ground-breaking finding published in *PNAS* (*Proceedings of the National Academy of Sciences*) and *Nature*, established credibility, quite literally rewrote biology textbooks and piqued scientists' curiosity.[2]

---

[2] Wim Hof Method, "The Science Behind the Wim Hof Method." Available at: https://www.wimhofmethod.com/science.

Since then, Wim has continued to submit himself and his method for scientific study. OK, so here's the bit I'd been waiting for. What made the Radbound study ground-breaking was that it aimed to test whether the results from the first study on Wim could be reproduced with a larger group.

Get this. This was a scientific peer reviewed paper published in the *Proceedings of National Academy of Sciences*. They brought in two groups. One group used one of Wim Hof's techniques. You know the one; well, you do if you joined in Chapter 2, and did the 30-breath challenge. I'm not kidding. We'll come back to that shortly, but that's all they did. They repeated that respiratory protocol for 15 minutes whilst the other group did nothing. Both groups were injected with E. coli. Yeah I know, crazy right? The second group all got fever, diarrhoea, and vomiting. All of them. The people who did the breathwork experienced none of the symptoms. *None of them.* Now, I appreciate that this all seems a bit extreme. "I only want to hit my sales target, Jim, not participate in Frankenstein experiments." I understand. Hang in there; nobody will be harmed in the reading of this book! For those inclined, you can read the clinical data from Radbound at Wimhofmethod.com; for the rest of us, let's make sense of all this and connect it to the achievement of whatever it is that you've got planned in the adventures that lie ahead.

I've overloaded this introduction with evidence. Some might say unnecessarily. I did so, because the two techniques used to take back control of our autonomic response are so simple, so unbelievably straightforward, that you might otherwise dismiss them as ridiculous. If I'd gone straight in and said the Wim Hof method could be broken down to two things: (1) a breathing exercise that takes five minutes and (2) a two-minute cold shower several times a week, then I have a feeling I would have lost the room. "No wonder he saved this for the end of the book, the bloke is clearly stark-raving bonkers!"

Here is the gist of it. Wim's ability to adapt his mind and body is largely dependent on variations of these two techniques that enable him to remain calm and composed, and thereby self-regulate his stress response. The result is he has access to his brain's cognitive functions rather than losing control and tipping him into a fight-or-flight response.

When you think about what it will take to achieve your aim-high goals, there will no doubt be certain circumstances that will be particularly demanding. How we respond to such stressful situations can be make or break. It might be preparing and delivering a pitch to investors or a presentation to prospective clients. It may be staying focused and resourceful when dealing with setbacks or when having to engage in courageous conversations. The various technical skills required will, of course, be unique to us and specific to our own aspirations, but the ability to remain calm and alert in the face of adversity is the same for all.

This is where it gets particularly exciting. For all our differences, one thing that we all share is our autonomic nervous system, and we all have it within us to use these techniques to help us regulate its response when under pressure.

Anyone recognise this? Work. Work. Work. Work. Holiday. Sick as a dog!

We don't need to be reminded of the negative effects of stress, however, there is one particular benefit that is worth highlighting. Stress is often misunderstood as some sort of ancient carryover. It sometimes gets lumped in with anxiety and depression, like it's a flaw in our design. But actually, if used effectively, stress has a particularly beneficial feature that we can tap into.

When we talk about stress in this context, we're not talking about raging amounts of cortisol. Cortisol has its functions too. A cortisol pulse when we wake clears our blurry eyes and gets us out of bed, but as we've mentioned earlier, less is more when it comes to cortisol. No, we're talking here about an effective amount of adrenaline in our body. Anytime we liberate adrenaline into our bloodstream, we also protect ourselves against infection of bacteria and viruses because, in fact, it activates our immune system. Handy, all things considered!

Think of it this way. Back in the day, if we had to go out and gather food for the family, which I'm guessing on occasion may have been a long and challenging process, you couldn't afford to get sick. The agitation and mild but continuous stress would provoke a persistent release of adrenaline, which not only provided energy, but it would also keep us from falling down sick. This ingenious system has got a hint of *superhuman* about it. But as they say, what goes up must come down!

I suspect we've all had times in our life when we've pushed ourselves a little too far. Cramming for an exam or getting to the end of a challenging project at work or frankly working from home whilst Home Schooling and getting dinner on the table day in, day out. Finally, when you get a few days R&R, nothing and no one harassing you, you come crashing down with an almighty head cold. This school of thought suggests that once we're back in our comfort zone and the stress is switched off, the Adrenaline goes with it. The adrenaline that was activating our immune system, delaying the inevitable consequences of not taking care of ourselves, but effectively keeping us in the game!

Somewhere within this example is the seed of a superhuman strategy.

Breathwork. It is and it does!

It's rare that people talk about breathing. We tend to think of sleep, nutrition, and exercise as the summary of our approach to health. Breathing is so underrated but so important. Since The Iceman stopped me in my tracks more than two years ago, I've used his method religiously as part of my morning routine. Above all else, I believe the conditioning effect it had on my respiratory system was responsible, more than any other single factor, for the successful completion of the triathlon. To push myself for more than 12 hours straight and not be out of breath at any point, still blows my mind. I'd say it was magic, except we know that's not the case. It was pure strategy. I haven't asked my nearest and dearest, but I'm sure they'd confirm that I've become a breathwork bore. In the past if you'd asked me about my breathing, I would have considered you odd. If you'd suggested I need to practice it, well, really? I mean who practice their breathing? Of all the things we have to work at in life, surely breathing is the one thing we've got nailed! We've all put in way more than the proverbial 10,000 hours. James Nestor might have something to say about that. His book, called simply *Breath*,[3] was an eye-opener and will give you all you'll ever need to know on the topic. If tapping into our inner superhuman is the objective, breathwork protocols are quite simply a must.

It's important to know that there's a neural circuit in our brainstem that connects to this muscle in your gut, the diaphragm, and the diaphragm does two things. It's not just used to move your lungs and help you breathe. It also sends signals back to your brain about the state of your body and controls your brain state. When you slow your breathing, your brain slows down. When you speed it up, your brain speeds up. You have muscles all over your body that were designed to do things like walk and pick up objects, and so on, but you only have one organ in your body that was designed to be consciously moved and that's your diaphragm. The diaphragm wasn't accidentally made to be under our conscious control. It's *absolutely* designed for conscious control. It's a very powerful part of our physiology and we should all be practicing with it.

Wim Hof's power-breathing technique has, in fact, been around for hundreds, if not thousands, of years, and is otherwise known as Tummo breathing or Pranayama. Tummo, which literally means "inner fire," is an ancient meditation technique practiced by monks in Tibetan Buddhism. Tummo consists of a combination of breathing and visualisation techniques used to enter a deep state of meditation that is used to increase a person's "inner heat." Yoga enthusiasts will be familiar with pranayama.

In Sanskrit, *prana* means "life energy" and *yama* means "control." The practice of pranayama involves breathing exercises and patterns. You purposely inhale, exhale, and hold your breath in a specific sequence. In yoga, pranayama is used with

[3] Nestor, J., (2021), *Breath: The New Science of a Lost Art*, Penguin Life.

other practices like physical postures (asanas) and meditation (dhyana).

Wim's genius lies in his ability to make these practices accessible to all comers. No kaftans required. I remember him being asked, "Bearing in mind the filtering benefits of nasal breathing, is it better to breathe in through the nose or the mouth," to which he replied, "Any hole will do!"

Whichever name we give it, the fundamental purpose is to stimulate a release of adrenaline, it's not designed to reduce stress. It's actually designed to increase our level of alertness and the technique of taking 30 or so full breaths with a breath hold at the end does exactly that. The focus is on an extended inhale. It's the opposite of the physiological sigh, that we covered in the section on stress busting where the focus was on an extended exhale. It makes perfect sense. This power-breathing technique is designed to raise the ceiling on our stress threshold. And what I mean by that is, throughout the day, we're confronted with moments that are stress-inducing, anything from the news headlines to never-ending to-do lists. The mind plays an important role in interpreting whether or not they're overwhelming or tolerable. So, intense breathing, or for that matter intense exercise or ice baths and cold showers, recondition the mind to be comfortable in these higher stress states. Effectively they provide a safe space to learn how to be calm in the mind when your body is full of adrenaline. It's basically stress inoculation.

A cold shower a day keeps the doctor away

Claims for the health benefits of cold-water immersion date back centuries. According to Hippocrates, water therapy allayed lassitude, and Thomas Jefferson used a cold foot bath every morning for six decades to "maintain his good health." Largely anecdotal evidence extols the virtues of cold-water swimming as a means of improving well-being. These health benefits are believed to be a consequence of the physiological responses and with repeated bouts, adaptive responses develop that may also impact our health. Interestingly, seaside resorts were founded on the perceived health benefits of sea swimming and the hazards associated with this health benefit led to the introduction of lifeguards.

Recently, there has been a significant growth in the number of people engaging in open, cold-water swimming, in terms of both competitions, ice swimming, marathon swimming, winter swimming, triathlon, and general wild swimming. With increased participation has come renewed and enthusiastic claims for the physiological and psychological health benefits. The claim is that gradual exposure to the cold starts a cascade of health benefits, including the buildup of something called brown adipose tissue, resulting in fat loss, reduced inflammation, balanced hormone levels, and improved sleep quality as well as the production of endorphins, the feel-good chemicals that naturally elevate our mood. Perhaps best of all, it provides a healthy, sustained increase in dopamine, and not just in the moment; it's been shown to stay in our system for hours afterwards.

It's important here to establish some safety parameters. First of all, getting into very, very cold water (−1°C, 30°F, or so) could put somebody into a state of cold-water shock. Not good. So, I'm talking cold showers, not frozen lakes. The temperature you can tolerate will depend on how cold-water adapted you are. That said, no matter how adapted you become, getting into cold water will always evoke a release of adrenaline. It never fails to take your breath away!

The question is, is it worth all the fuss?

There was an interesting study in the *European Journal of Applied Physiology*.[4] Researchers looked at people getting exposed to water that was warm, moderately cold or very cold: 32°C (90°F), 20°C (68°F), or 14°C (57°F). Upon getting into cold water, the

---

[4] Srámek, P., Simecková, M., Janský, L., Savlíková, J., and Vybíral, S., (2000), "Human Physiological Responses to Immersion into Water of Different Temperatures," *European Journal of Applied Physiology*, March, 81(5): 436–442. doi:10.1007/s004210050065.

changes in adrenaline were immediate and fast. Everybody experiences a huge increase in adrenaline. Whether it's your first time or your 1,001 time. More interestingly, researchers observed that dopamine levels started to rise slowly, and then continue to rise and reach levels as high as 2.5 times above baseline.

The increase in dopamine from cold water exposure was similar to what one sees from cocaine, except unlike a rapid rise and crash, the cold water triggers a slow release and a long arc, meaning the sustained rise in dopamine took up to three hours to come back down to baseline.

So, just like the power breathing, cold-water exposure turns out to be a very potent stimulus for shifting our mind and body to a state of readiness. This would probably explain why so many people combine both practices to form their morning routine. My own experience aside, which has been a significant uplift in energy and composure as I head into my day, feedback from friends, colleagues, and clients alike has been, without exception, dramatic to say the least. That said, with these two performance and well-being hacks the only way to judge is by your own results!

Running your own experiment—Adapt more to endure less

Aside from the increases in dopamine, many people use deliberate cold exposure to stimulate metabolism, reduce inflammation, and for resilience training. One lesser-known tool is to be sure that you continuously move your body while in the water. Movement breaks up the thermal layer around your body, makes it even colder, and causes the release of even more adrenaline, which is the primary stimulus for the positive effects of deliberate cold exposure. The takeaway is to get the most out of it by keeping your mind still whilst moving throughout.

More benefits without having to stay in longer. So, music on and dance the hoochie koo!

In a nutshell, jump straight into the cold if building resilience is your priority. Alternate warm and cold for cardiovascular health. Both approaches are good for metabolism, fat burning, and if you're looking for a boost to your immune system. As with everything there is an element of trial and error and a period of adjustment. Listen to your body and find your feet!

Iceman challenge

During the process of adaptation start warm, inject a little cold, then back to warm.
Days 1 to 5: Cold for 10 seconds
Days 6 to 10: Cold for 20 seconds
Days 11 to 15: Cold for 30 seconds
Days 16 to 20: Cold for 45 seconds
Days 21 to 25: Cold for one minute
Days 26 to 30: Cold for between one and two minutes

Power-breathing respiratory protocol: When, where, and how often?

Many people include three or four rounds of this breathwork practice as part of their morning routine. It's a great way to start the day and is perfect preparation for your cold shower. Equally, it works as a powerful way to prepare for an important call if working from home. It flushes our tension and provokes a calm and alert state of mind.

Even taking five minutes and doing just one round will take you up a notch or two. You can use the QR code in chapter 2, to see a demonstration of this exercise, detailed again on the next page, or visit my website jimsteele.com for more information.

The Exercise

Part one

Sit comfortably or lie down.

Take in 30 full, deep breaths. Fully in then let go. Fully in then let go. No gap between exhale and inhale. Make it circular. Feeling light-headed or tingling sensations are normal. Keep going, fully in and let go. About the same effort level as a fast walk. We're looking for focused but not forced. After the 30th breath, you breathe out and STOP.

Don't breathe back in, just relax and hold.

Part two

Wait calmly until you feel the need to breathe back in. You may surprise yourself with how long you can comfortably pause. When you do feel the urge to breathe back in, take one full recovery breath (stop the stopwatch), hold your breath for the count of 15, and enjoy!

Some FAQs

Should I breathe in through my mouth or nose?

Whichever is more comfortable. Mix it up a bit. The objective is simply to take in full breaths.

Can I do this whilst on the move?

Nope. Sitting or lying down only. The more comfortable you are the better the result. As you over-oxygenate, it's normal to experience light-headedness. Enjoyable when you're sitting comfortably, not particularly helpful when driving or operating heavy machinery.

Does it have to be exactly 30 breaths?

No, although 30 to 35 seems to be an optimal number.

Should I breathe fast or slow?

Faster is more energising, whilst slower is more relaxing. I'd suggest steady, full inhales for the count of two or three. When you exhale, you don't need to fully exhale, just let it fall out, nice and easy.

OK, let's do it!

For maximum effect, I would encourage three rounds. The first round is to get used to it.

The second round is to practice relaxing into the process, and then the third round is for real!

Time the breath hold on the third round. Enjoy.

Note: This exercise is not advised if you're pregnant or if you have any pulmonary conditions.

For those that would like to take a deeper look into Wim Hof's method, he has a wealth of information on his website. I have no affiliation or financial incentive to point you in his direction, but for me it has and continues to be a terrific source of inspiration.

These techniques have been pivotal in my journey over the last few years. I wouldn't dream of not injecting some cold into my shower and, as for the power breathing, it's so versatile I could have included it in a number of the chapters.

It's a demonstration for tapping potential: Chapter 3

It's a stress buster: Chapter 8

It's an entry to flow: Chapter 10

It's a mindfulness practice: Chapter 14

It's deep meditation: Chapter 14

It's an active recovery strategy: Chapter 16

It's a primer to kick-start an exercise routine: Chapter 17

Safe to say this simple superhuman hack will still be with me long into the future. The reason being it's now just one of *my things*.

Chapter 19

TOP BOARDER THINGS

Figure 19.1 Do you dare?

Not many readers will recognise Cardiff's Empire Pool. Opened in 1958 and demolished to make way for Wales' Rugby mecca, the Millennium Stadium in 1998, it was the only Olympic-size pool in the country. Fifty metres (164 feet) from end to end, with five diving boards. Oh, those diving boards! One- and three-metre (3- and 10-foot) springy boards. Then came the platforms. The third board was 5 metres (16 feet) up, the fourth would take you to 7.5 metres (24.6 feet), and the board of all boards was, of course, Top board. Never referred to as the fifth board, always simply known as "Top!"

For an eager 10-year-old in 1974, hearing the words, "Coming to the Empire on Saturday?" would immediately set the heart racing. During school holidays it would have been a daily occurrence if pocket money had allowed. A significant amount of my early teens was spent standing on one of those diving boards. I emphasise *standing*. Not diving. Or, to be brutally honest, as being expertly demonstrated by the individual in Figure 19.1, sitting on the third board, waiting in the "consideration" position. You can just about pick him out, sitting alone with only his fear for company. Yep, that would have been me.

For many months we'd been happily diving off the two springy boards, 1 and 3 metres (1 and 3 feet). Very happy there. No ambition to climb higher. No ambition, that is, until one of my *friends* dived off third. Why? Why would they do that to me? Of course, this mean't what? That's right, I had to have a go. Had to, didn't want to. Big difference!

You start optimistically, looking up from the poolside and thinking, that doesn't look too bad. Your encouraging inner voice saying, "Come on, you'll be alright; you can do it." The illusion is soon destroyed after climbing that extra ladder and taking your first look over the edge. You've never seen the world from this perspective; there are no references to cling to. Just the handrail. Holding on for dear life. I wasn't consciously aware of it at the time, but I'm sure the overriding and overwhelming thought that dominated my thinking went something like, "OH MY GOD, WHAT IF I BECOME THE BOY?" You know the boy. Have you heard about the boy? Legend has it he dived off, belly flopped and split his stomach open. Blood filled the pool! You know, the boy!

It was just an urban myth. It never actually happened, but at that critical moment, in my mind, it seemed very real. What's more, it was about to happen *again*, to me. You may well have experienced something similar at a pool near you. As long as that's the thought dominating our focus, what can't we get ourselves to do?

No matter how much we want to jump, no matter how much we want to ask that challenging question in a meeting, to go for that promotion, or start our own business, we'll never move towards that negative perceived outcome. When the image of the impending future is so painful, physically or emotionally, our willpower simply can't compete. I want to make the move, but I just can't get myself to.

So, there I was, seated in the consideration position. I could say that my ambition was to dive off the third board, but actually my focus was being led by my real ambition, not getting hurt.

I'd like to say that I pulled myself together, snapped out of it, and propelled myself forth, but I didn't. No exaggeration, this went on for weeks. I remember one fruitless visit, when I spent the entirety of the allowed swimming time (a wrist band given on entry, denoted the start of your 60 minutes), fixed in the "consideration" seat trying to summon up the courage and follow Nike's advice to "Just Do It," when over the tannoy, they announced, "Green bands leave the pool." I climbed down the stairs and walked out. . .dry!

But then, one day, it all changed. Without knowing why, or how, I did it. I jumped. YEEEES! Did I go back up? Oh, yes. Did I pause the second time? Oh, no. Straight off. What moments before was nigh on impossible, is now effortless. No pause, straight off. Within four or five dives I'm even holding the swallow position. Next stop the Olympics!

Then, before you've barely had time to celebrate, what does your friend go and do? Yep, they dive off the fourth board! And the painful process repeats all over again. Here's the point. When you finally dive off the fourth board, do you ever go back down to the third board?

Of course not. But why not? No challenge back at the third board? No buzz down there anymore? Both good reasons. But not the real reason. The real reason you don't go back down to the third board is because now, I think you'll find you're a *fourth boarder*, and *fourth boarders* dive off the fourth board, not the third board. Who dives off the third board? That's right, the third boarders. Not you, not now, or ever again. It is, quite literally, beneath you. You're now a *fourth boarder*, and *fourth boarders* do *fourth boarder things*.

Only one thing left to do: Top Board.

But before we do, let's assess where we are. First, if you take only one thing from this story, take this: we never outperform our identity. In other words, the things we do, the way we behave, the books we read, the people we hang out with, our hobbies and interests, even the goals we set for ourselves are shaped by the person we see ourselves to be.

Let's consider a few of the things we've been looking at in *Unashamedly Superhuman*. For example, if I asked you, do you meditate? If the answer is yes, and I followed up by asking why, you could give me all of the reasons, or you could just round them up and say, "It's just my *thing*."

Again, I appreciate there are many reasons why we do or don't participate in certain activities, but at a fundamental level, the driving force is whether we see those things as part of who we are. Knowing this provides us with a terrific strategy for creating the change we want to see in our lives.

Assuming the right identity

OK, back to Empire Pool. In order to dive off Top, we have to assume the identity of being a top boarder. That's easy once we've dived off, but what if we could do that before we even climb the final ladder? Our objective is to align our identity to our new goal, not to our past achievements.

We have learned from our time on the previous diving boards that once we dived off the first time, on the third and fourth board, the seemingly impossible instantly became manageable. We can therefore rationalise that there is a strong possibility that will be the case on top boards. So, what can we do before we even walk up the final ladder, so that by the time we stand on the edge it will feel like we've been there before, successfully having got that first one under our belt? How can we develop the feeling we'll no doubt experience after we dive, but before we actually do?

Try this, imagine holding a lemon, a juicy, ripe, sour lemon. Go on, go with me. That's it, really use your imagination. What would it look like held out in front of you? Feel the waxy texture. As you squeeze it you can notice the juice rising. Now just bite into it. See if you can imagine sucking the lemon juice and notice what it would taste like if you could. OK, you can put your lemon down! Now let me ask you a question. Could you taste it?

Were you able to create a tangy taste in your mouth? Some of you will even have generated some saliva! Yet, there was no lemon. It's interesting to consider that the brain doesn't seem to know the difference between a real or a vividly imagined event.

Therefore, when we say "I am a top boarder" and visualise the things we would be doing if we were, that being diving off easily and successfully, our brain generates the reference of success and locks it in our mind. It matters not that it is imagined, it codes it the same as if it were real. It needs to be vividly imagined, and repeated a number of times, but each time the feeling becomes stronger and stronger and easy to access in the real world.

Now, does that mean we will definitely become top boarders? Maybe, maybe not, but it starts to put the odds in our favour of at least being able to summon up the resourcefulness required to step off the edge and move us towards the realisation of our aim-higher goal. Again, we never outperform our identity, but with this performance hack we're starting to shape our identity based on our potential and not on our past performances.

Identity in high-performing teams

I see this all the time with teams, particularly high-performing teams. In fact, my first introduction to international rugby was Wales versus Scotland at Cardiff Arms Park. I was 12. So was my mate, Basil, and my brother was a year older. We left the Empire Pool and walked next door to Cardiff Arms Park Stadium. It was the beginning of an obsession. We didn't know it then, but we were watching arguably the greatest rugby team in the history of the game. Wales was so good back in the day that for many years, at every game the question on everyone's lips wasn't *if* we were going to win, it was by how many points.

This was a high-performing team by anyone's standards. The players were all stars. I could name all 15 then as I could now. But it's not just me, any rugby fan of any age from anywhere in the world knows Gareth Edwards, Barry John, The Pontypool front row and my boyhood hero JPR. No name required, just initials! Madonna wouldn't even get away with just M! That's how big the rugby stars were in Wales. But this wasn't just a bunch of talented individuals, this was a team. They had that something extra. Some call it synergy, where the whole is greater than the sum of its parts. One plus one equals three or more! They inspired pride into a small nation of three million people, and on a cold Saturday afternoon watching them give everything they had, blood, sweat, and tears, made a 12-year-old feel 10-foot tall. Granted this was my team, and there is an outside chance that I may be biased or perhaps my glasses are a little rose-tinted.

Wherever you are in the world, I'm sure you have examples of your own, whether from the world of sports or otherwise. An orchestra playing in unison, an aerobatics display team performing with precision, or maybe it's a team of surgeons or first responders supporting each other to support us. So, what is that secret sauce, what creates the magic? What differentiates a team from just a group of very talented individuals?

Whenever I've had the opportunity to interview business people, and team leaders, in particular, that is the question I always begin with. Over the years you start to see the themes and patterns that separate good teams from great ones. Having a clear purpose or a common goal always comes up, a vision of the future that brings everyone together. Clear roles and responsibilities feature on most lists, as does having shared values to encourage cohesion as well as forging a culture that engenders transparency and trust. Facilitating open communication and giving honest feedback creates continuous and never-ending improvement and supports an agenda of personal and professional development. It's a great checklist and they all have a part to play but there is one thing I've repeatedly come across that seems to act as the glue that bonds people together and generates a tremendous amount of intrinsic motivation. It's the real reason everyone wants to stay in the team and why others want to join it. It's the team's brand or *identity*.

In terms of hitting long-term objectives, perhaps the one thing that destroys most cohesiveness in teams is when someone's not actually playing for the team. They're still playing for themselves. High-performing teams play for each other but more than that, they play for the jersey, so to speak. I mentioned that I had the opportunity to interview Kate Richardson Walsh, ex GB women's hockey captain, and her answer summed it up perfectly.

Kate told how she'd been in lots of great groups with very talented, skillful, and technically accomplished players, but they hadn't all excelled as teams. She said, "Even though we had mission statements and goals, and there may even have been a sense of alignment, it's the weaving of all of that into the fabric of who we are that makes the difference. That's when we truly became successful." She added that, "A team may have a vision and a mission statement with goals and declared values, but do they know what that means, day to day? Does every single person feel empowered to drive it, to own it, to be accountable for it? Do they know behaviourally what is expected of them and their teammates? Effectively do they know what it means to be in *this* team? To participate in a way that exemplifies what *this* team stands for?"

When we're clear about what our team wants to be known for, we're able to challenge ourselves and each other against that overriding search for excellence, every single day. When we get to that point, we don't roll up to a business pitch, or the Olympic Games for that matter, and just rely on the star players to bring it home. It's every single person, every single day. What's more, when the brand of the team is bigger than any individual, you attract and welcome diversity. You want differences of opinion, different experiences, different points of view because that healthy friction will bring about greater solutions to find ways to win. It's about continuing to build the brand identity together. The objective is to leave it a better team than you found it. High-performing teams do high-performing things. Most natural thing in the world. It's just *their thing!*

So, what if we took this winning principle of creating an identity for everyone to live up to, and applied it to ourselves. Like we said, top boarders do top boarder things, it's not an effort, it's the most natural thing in the world.

Cultivating an identity that defines us based on our potential and not just on our past results is a concept that can be applied to more than high-performing teams or moving up the diving board hierarchy. Equally it applies to moving ahead in our careers. I'm a manager. I'm a team leader. I'm a project lead. I'm a business owner. I'm an entrepreneur, or in the superhero case of Mr Tony Stark. . .I AM IRONMAN.

Such identity statements switch on our internal seeking system, causing us to not only see opportunities that would otherwise slip by unnoticed, but it also puts a spotlight on the actions and behaviours required to move us in the direction of our goals. Furthermore, we start to frame those habits and behaviours as our own. They become *our thing*. The very things that we may have avoided doing in the past become the most natural things in the world.

There comes a point when we no longer have to try to create our winning habits. No more need to consciously remove the friction and grease the wheels to enable us to effortlessly close the gap between common sense and common practice. It's just us. It's what we do. We know it, and before long everyone knows it. So, as we draw to the end of this section on becoming stronger by tapping into our physiology, what are you going to make *your thing*? How will your mission-critical goals benefit from having an endless supply of energy? How about becoming the go-to person for habit stacking by mastering how to align emotion, logic, and brain chemicals? Or maybe recovery will be your new thing. Plugged into your biometrics and known for factoring in active and micro recovery breaks to boost your performance.

Your thing may support one of the big three to thrive. Achieving world-class sleep stats or an approach to nutrition that fuels you all day long or adopting a morning routine that ticks your exercise box and supports your sporting aspirations.

Or maybe Wim's method is your thing. Becoming the go-to person on breathwork and respiratory protocols and being the cold shower person? Or maybe you'll clear out your closet and refill it with a selection of barefoot shoes and become the rewilding type? Anyway, you get the idea.

Let me finish with this. Wrestling with an upgraded identity is perhaps the most challenging version of swimming against the current. When I was offered a book deal and invited to pen my thoughts on how to tap into our in-built potential, mindset, and physiology, I had a mini identity crisis. Write a book, me? My thoughts flashed back to a nervous 15-year-old opening my GCSE exam results; 12 exams sat, one passed. An A grade. In art! An extra year in the sixth form produced four more, all grade *C*. One of them was English language. My English literature grade was classified a *U*. Unclassified to be exact.

I think you have to spell your name wrong to get a *U*. So, forgive me for a moment of self-congratulations, but I believe it's important to celebrate one's successes. At the start of this project, I wrote something on a Post-it® note and stuck it on the screen of my laptop. It was a declaration of intent, and I didn't know for sure that it wasn't a tad delusional. However, as I power down my Apple Mac, I'm claiming it as fact.

I am an author.

Chapter 20

IRONMAN® ATHLETE. TO BE OR NOT TO BE THAT IS THE QUESTION

I feel this is the appropriate time to put to bed my *IRONMAN®
triathlon* story. For my triathlon challenge the outcome was
clear. My mountain was becoming an *IRONMAN®* athlete, based
on the distance and rules set out by the sport's governing body.
Deciding my highest priorities had been decided for me too. I'd
been challenged to develop a training programme that would
enable people to combine high performance and well-being.
One out of two wouldn't do. My definition of *high performance*
was to complete the distance faster than the international average for the distance, and well-being meant feeling better at the
end of the day than I did at the beginning. And when I say "feel
better" I don't mean happier, I mean physically – structurally
free from injury and all achieved within my optimum heart rate.
The Whoop stats wouldn't lie.

The average finishing time for males of all age groups, stated
by RunTri[1] based on an analysis of more than 41,000 finishers,
was 12 hours and 35 minutes. I've learned that triathletes are
typically super focused on their times, and why wouldn't they be;
it's the perfect measure of their progress whilst providing focus
and motivation, both of which attract flow! I can't claim to be
part of what I believe are a tremendously disciplined group of
athletes. This was my one and only experience of dipping my toe
in their world. Although I took a tremendous amount of inspiration from podcasts like *Crushing Iron*, and some invaluable training tips from a coach at Training Peaks, I decided to train alone.
I hadn't anticipated having to complete the distance on
my own too!

Following my tumble off the bike I restarted my training in
October 2019, having signed up for a trip to Houston to take on
IRONMAN® Texas in April 2020. Flight's booked and raring to
go. Well, we all know what happened next. Even rolling over my

---

[1] Britt, R., "How Much Time Does It Take to Finish An Average
Ironman Triathlon? Average Ironman Finish Times," *RunTri*. Available
at: https://www.runtri.com/2011/06/how-long-does-it-take-to-finish-
ironman.html#:~:text=How%20long%20does%20it%20take,26.2%
20miles%20in%204%3A54.

starting place for April 2021 was to no avail due to COVID cancellations. This was supposed to be a 12-month goal and here I was two years later questioning if I had the motivation to wait another year. However, the undeniable benefit of what was now three failed attempts to get to the start line, was two more years of barefoot running, two more years of daily cold showers, two more years of daily breathwork practices, two more years fine-tuning my nutritional strategy. The performance and well-being *hacks* were doing their job, and from the inside out I felt indestructible.

Note: I feel I should just touch on the barefoot thing.

Swimming against the current

We introduced this idea in Chapter 6 when we talked about activating the new and improved. The point then was that in the pursuit of our adventures we're likely to be confronted by the reality that our current knowledge, skills, processes, or mindsets are not going to be enough. Adopting any new behaviour involves an element of going against our current approach. That's the challenge with change and why it's easy to resist. When it comes to tapping into our physiology, I'm going to introduce a game-changing change, which for me at least took this to a whole new level. Swimming against the current recognises that sometimes the route to a game-changing strategy can initially require a complete detachment from not only your current viewpoint but the views of almost everyone you know. That said, since when did *they* know best? History is littered with examples of how so-called experts got things very, very wrong.

"The phone has too many flaws to be seriously considered as a means of communication." —Western Union statement, 1876

"I think there is a world market for maybe five computers." — Thomas Watson, Chairman IBM, 1943

"We do not like their sound, and guitar music is on its way out of fashion." The biggest mistake by Decca Recording when turning away the Beatles in 1962.

"There is no reason why someone would want a computer in their home." —Ken Olson, President and founder of Digital Devilment, 1977

Take a minute to consider how this provocative principle may relate to you. Is there a current blind spot, hiding an opportunity of a lifetime?

While you ponder that, indulge me as I explain how finding mine not only enabled me to cruise through the marathon phase of the IRONMAN® triathlon injury-free, but also, I believe, set me up for a pain-free future.

Allow me to introduce Tony Riddle. He recently ran the length of the United Kingdom barefoot! That's 30 miles (48 km) a day back-to-back for 30 days. During my recovery from the bike incident, I attended one of his talks. During the 12 months leading up to the crash, my run training had focused on just putting in the hard yards on the road. Yes, I was becoming fitter and stronger, but far and away the greatest gains I was achieving was in a steady uplift in pain. Knees, hips, back, all creaking under the strain. Regular trips to the chiropractor and a constant supply of anti-inflammatory medication were just about seeing me through. Superhuman? Not even close.

I'm sure you're familiar with Einstein's often-quoted definition of *insanity*. "Doing the same thing over and over and expecting different results." That was me. Undeniably, the results I was getting could only be a direct result of the things I was doing, but what other options were there? Running is running; it hurts, right? So, when I heard Tony state that structurally everyone is capable of running pain-free, I wanted to be excited. In fact, he enthused, we're built for it. I appreciated his optimism, but clearly, he didn't understand my body. It was different for me. My medical history would suggest that structurally I couldn't run without getting hurt. My surgeon said so! Skip ahead six months and I'm running at least one half-marathon a week barefoot. No pain. No injury. No problem. No going back. I mention this purely as a metaphor. Swimming against the current isn't easy. Challenging our beliefs and adopting new approaches that, in spite of the evidence, seem ludicrous is difficult at best. Even when our past strategies have continued to fail to deliver the results we want, if that is all we know that is all we will continue to use. So, how does this barefoot thing work? Intuitively, surely running barefoot will only make matters worse. The more cushion in the sole of the trainers the better. Big and bouncy is best, right? Wrong. Couldn't be more wrong. Running barefoot demands that you change your style of running. You can't heel strike, that would be painful. So, you change, and you change quickly. Suddenly your feet wake up and start doing the job they were meant to do. Slowly but surely, they start to spread out and adapt to the ground beneath you. Ligaments and tendons lighting up and being employed for the first time since running in just your socks on sports day when you were eight! Even then we knew there was something good about kicking off the pumps. With practice and patience, soon enough I started to experience zero pressure on my knees or lower back. The feet were loving the extra responsibility. The ankles unlocked and even the hips joined the party, as they are designed to do.

Anecdotal evidence to one side, there is ample scientific data to back this up for those interested. A great place to start would be Adharanand Finn's book *Running with the Kenyans*.[2]

It took me 56 years to find out that we have this in-built system that can enable us to run pain-free, but seeing was believing. Or perhaps believing is seeing is a more appropriate turn of phrase. Of course, I wish I'd found out 30 years earlier—30 years of a repeated pattern of failure . . . Exercise. Injury. Hospital. Recover. Repeat. That said, better late than never. Same body, dramatically different strategy equalled dramatic improvements in physical capability. Which was most welcome, after all I had an IRONMAN® triathlon to complete.

I now regularly ask the question, what else is possible? What else don't we know about our own mind and body that could enable us to achieve the seemingly impossible?

---

[2] Finn, A., (2013), *Running with the Kenyans: Discovering the Secrets of the Fastest People on Earth*, Faber & Faber, Main edition.

Barefoot running is niche, and I'm not trying to sell you on the idea. I've sold my kids on the idea, and when I took my grandson for his first pair of shoes, Vivo Barefoot in Covent Garden was a no-brainer, but each to their own on this one. For most people, this one is more like swimming against the tsunami. Treat it merely as a metaphor for looking for step change as opposed to marginal gains.

Of course, I wanted to prove myself in a sanctioned IRONMAN® event but as that tap had been turned off, I decided I'd just have to go it alone. Some might say that doesn't count. Not just some, me included. You're only an IRONMAN® athlete when you cross the finish line in under 17 hours and the announcer shouts, "JIM STEELE, YOU ARE AN IRONMAN® ATHLETE."

On 2 September 2021, it was only about the distance. I arrived at Caversham lakes at 6 a.m. in the dark, where they have the 2.4 miles (3.9 km) marked out. Next, I rode up and down a section of the A4 near Reading for 112 miles (180 km), dropped off the bike, then back to the A4 to run the 26.2-mile (42.2-km) route that I'd marked out. A group of friends and a couple of clients tracked me all day on an app called Runkeeper. I felt having proof would be a good thing. A handful of friends and family were waiting at the finish line 12 hours and 23 minutes later, also in the dark. I suppose in some ways going solo was easier as there were no other swimmers climbing all over me or any distractions to knock me off my stride. Not much pressure either other than knowing the trackers would wonder what was happening if I pulled over on the bike for a quick nap! Although in other ways it was more demanding. There was no hubbub to fire up the adrenaline or cheering crowds to bring me home on the latter stages of a punishing run. I did, however, have my nearest and dearest pop up every couple of hours at various points on the course to provide a much-needed shot in the arm.

Anyway, when all is said and done, officially or otherwise, I'm satisfied that I climbed my mountain. I carved out a strategy and executed a detailed plan of action, and proved to myself that there's plenty of life left in the old dog yet.

Chapter 21

NOW RISE UP

Around the start of 2009 a news programme was holding a debate about the global financial crisis. The leading question was: "How is it possible to lift morale in such unprecedented circumstances?" Several experts were there to share their views.

One of the panel was an ex-RAF pilot. I guess the correlation was something along the lines of how can we keep our heads and get ourselves out of a seemingly impossible situation. He talked about a particular sortie whereby he found himself flying into a combat zone, which consisted of his plane and that of four enemy aircraft.

"How did you feel when you realised your predicament?" he was asked.

"Focused," he replied.

"Surely, the fact that you were outnumbered four to one must have negatively impacted your morale?" the interviewer continued.

"All I can tell you is I remained calm and confident."

"But the chances of being shot down. You were outnumbered four to one."

After a short pause the pilot concluded, "I didn't see it like that. I considered it to be a target-rich environment!"

Got to love his confidence. The point being that when you know deep down that you have everything you need to meet the demands that lie ahead, you back yourself and life becomes target rich.

The key is to lean into that mindset. Believe in yourself and your inner resources. If you test them, you'll know they're there whenever you need them.

You have a choice

It's not only what happens to us that will make the difference in our lives. What determines the true difference is how we're able to choose our response. *Unashamedly Superhuman* sits in the gap between stimulus and response.

The performance hacks I've shared in this book give us a chance to regroup between that stimulus and our response. They allow us to reset and respond with conscious thought, rather than just reacting. As that gap between stimulus and response widens for you, it creates the space you need to make a conscious choice. The more you use the conditioning techniques I've shared, the more and more resourceful your responses to different stimuli will be.

More than that though, you're also learning how to control the stimulus itself. You can use the hacks here to choose your own biochemistry and that makes the stimulus you receive in each situation your choice as well. Tapping into your superhuman abilities is, above all else, about regaining control.

There's no magic involved in being superhuman. Hopefully by this stage you've realised that. These abilities aren't supernatural, they're super natural. They are Mother Nature's gift to us all.

Adventure lies ahead

As we mentioned earlier in the book, adventures provide all sorts of opportunities, not just the chance to achieve our goals, but also the many learning experiences that we'll no doubt have along the way.

Maybe you're right in the middle of an adventure and *Unashamedly Superhuman* is providing a timely pause, a chance to regroup and take on some additional resources. Or maybe you're still at base camp, planning your route ahead and the component parts of Better, Smarter, Stronger are preparing you for what's coming.

None of us know what the future holds, but I can promise you one thing: it'll be an adventure.

What's more, it doesn't so much matter what adventures lie ahead; what matters most is that you're prepared. By fine-tuning your superhuman abilities through the various hacks and strategies in this book, you will be ready.

We now know we have within us the ability to become Better. We learned:

A.D.A.P.T.

Accept our adventure with cognitive reframing.

Direct our seeking system to open our eyes to new possibilities.

Activate the new and improved to take us to the next level.

Persist by suppressing the quit reflex.

Tune in and tune up to carve out new skills.

We sharpened our awareness of the world around us and learned how to adapt more in order to endure less. We found a way to control our potential, and tap into it at will.

It's the first element of being *Unashamedly Superhuman.*

To become Smarter, we learned:

F.O.C.U.S.

Flow follows focus, causing us to feel and perform at our very best.

One, two, three minds shifts us from negative to positive to flow states.

Cycle to flow gives us the process to push through our comfort zones.

Under the radar creates limitless motivation.

Stay in the now develops composure and laser-like focus.

You know how to unlock the part of your mind that enables you to tap into a high-performance mindset where you both feel and perform at your very best.

Then, we became Stronger. We learned:

H.A.B.I.T.

Habit stacking gives us total control over our winning behaviours.

Active recovery helps us to reset and keeps us in the game for longer.

Big three to thrive generates endless energy.

Iceman cometh restrengthens our nervous system and builds unstoppable endurance.

Top boarder things shows us how to shape our identity to drive long-term change.

We found ways to harness new energy and build up endurance. There's a boxing gym in London called Jab, and its tagline is, "We don't work out, we train." When you train, there's a purpose behind what you're doing. This purpose drives you to become Stronger than you thought possible.

Accept that you, too, are superhuman

We've explored tools and techniques that give us access to a readily available, in-built system of human resources. We've focused on what it is to be Better by tapping into our potential Smarter by tapping into our mindset, and Stronger by tapping into our physiology.

Let there be no doubt: we all have superpowers and these powers open the door to the more that we all seek.

Now you know you have these resources inside you, what identity will you choose?

What does *Unashamedly Superhuman* mean to you?

Most important of all, what are you going to do with your newly discovered superpowers?

You have your cape, now rise up and fly.

About the Author

Jim Steele is a business speaker, executive coach, leadership facilitator, and one of the world's top business performance pioneers. Having gained experience at various levels of the organisational ladder, Jim understands the wide variety of challenges people face at every level in any business. He has dedicated his career to finding practical and achievable solutions to these challenges.

Drawing from cutting-edge neuroscientific research, Jim is always seeking new solutions for the ever-evolving challenges in today's fast-paced business world. He has a particular passion for combining high performance with well-being, the basis of this book and his *Unashamedly Superhuman* program.

Jim has spent more than two decades helping clients across Europe, the Middle East, and the United States deliver on their performance and growth objectives, but above all his practical strategies that blend high performance and well-being improve his clients' resilience and deliver demonstrable results.

To dive deeper into becoming Better, Smarter, Stronger, and owning being *Unashamedly Superhuman*, visit Jim's website: www .jimsteele.com. You'll find resources to help you unlock untapped potential and connect this to your goals. You can also find out more about how to focus on the practical elements of becoming *Unashamedly Superhuman* by accessing Jim's online course and/or contacting him about tailored coaching programs and speaking engagements.

Index

Page numbers followed by *f* refer to figures.